"For twenty-three years, I have observed Bishop McBath's leadership ascent. As he shares his remarkable insights, you will learn to succeed at the Next Level with growing integrity and character. In a day when people are searching for effective leadership, Bishop McBath is a bright light on the horizon."

—Bishop Richard Hilton, Senior Pastor,
Calvary Church, Johnson City, Tennessee

"B. Courtney McBath is a true leader with tremendous vision. In his book, *Living at the Next Level*, he perfectly illustrates what it means to have a successful life in God—one that is full of joy, no matter the circumstances. B. Courtney McBath is a man of God who desires for you to live a fulfilled life. Get this book, and prepare for your life to be radically changed!"

—John Bevere, Author/Speaker, Messenger International,
Colorado Springs/Australia/United Kingdom

"If anyone knows about Next Level living, Courtney McBath does. In his own unique and powerful way, he has given us a literary work that arrests us in our quest for fulfillment through the attainment of externals, while freeing us to find true fulfillment through an intimate relationship with God. It takes one with a heart for God and a mind like Bishop McBath's to show us, scripturally, how to live at the Next Level, no matter what state we find ourselves in. This book is a must-read for those of us who are ready to truly live at the Next Level for the rest of our lives."

—Cynthia L. Hale, Senior Pastor, Ray of Hope Christian Church

"Many people are living for tomorrow and missing out on today. Courtney McBath has written a book that challenges us to embrace what is ours right now—a rich life of friendship with God. Don't miss this book!"

—Gary D. Chapman, Ph.D., Author of *The Five Love Languages* and *The Five Languages of Apology*

"I have known Courtney McBath since his seminary days at the Regent University School of Divinity, where I was his dean. He was a bright and earnest student of God's Word who showed tremendous promise. Since those days, he has fulfilled his destiny by drawing thousands to what has become the largest megachurch in Tidewater, Virginia. His book, *Living at the Next Level,* reveals the insight and power of his preaching. This is an amazing book by an amazing man."

—Vinson Synan, Dean Emeritus, Regent University School of Divinity

"I have known Dr. B. Courtney McBath as a friend, colleague, brother, client, and a major encourager in my life for many years. To all who know Dr. McBath, this book is no surprise: he is always communicating this book's concepts. *Living at the Next Level* is an overflow of who Dr. McBath is, and it will capture your imagination about who you are in God and how you can experience life at the Next Level every day. Are you ready for the journey?"

—Dr. Samuel R. Chand, President, Samuel R. Chand Consulting

"James records in scripture that Abraham was called the friend of God. What a remarkable statement! Does that concept seem foreign to you? Are you a friend of God? In his book, *Living at the Next Level*, B. Courtney McBath shows believers how God's friendship is extended to all of His children. Through vivid scriptural stories, McBath illustrates how living and reveling in the friendship of God provides us with the ultimate joy and satisfaction in life … God himself!"

—Dr. R. Kirk Nowery, Chief Operating Officer, Samaritan's Purse

"B. Courtney McBath is one of the most dynamic people I've ever met. His teachings are biblically sound yet culturally relevant. He has a phenomenal ability to positively shape the thinking of others, both as a one-on-one mentor and as a minister to thousands. This book centers on what has become a mantra of modern society: 'The Next Level.' Through this book, McBath unlocks the mystery of the Next Level and how to live there. This book is destined to change countless lives!"

—Teresa Hairston, Publisher, *Gospel Today* Magazine

"In a world obsessed with the accumulation of money and possessions as a benchmark for moving up, Dr. McBath gives us the keys to the Next Level. Through the life of Peter, we can see that the Next Level is not about external progress, but rather about the process of surrendering to God. This is a matter of focus, not position."

—Susie C. Owens, Co-Pastor, Greater Mt. Calvary Holy Church, Washington, D.C.

"Whether life teases us or we tease ourselves, seldom in life are we satisfied. B. Courtney McBath's book, *Living at the Next Level*, doesn't dodge our frustrations but attacks them head-on. Always talking to us where we live, McBath takes our hand and walks us through an understanding of principles that will help us embrace the journey of life. As some say, "The victory is the journey," and that is what the Next Level is about."

—Dr. Clarence Shuler, President/CEO,
Building Lasting Relationships, Inc.

Scripture quotations marked KJV are taken from the King James Version of the Bible. Public domain. | Scripture quotations marked NIV are taken from the Holy Bible, New International Version®, NIV®. Copyright © 1973, 1978, 1984, 2011 by Biblica, Inc.™ Used by permission of Zondervan. All rights reserved worldwide. www.zondervan.com. The "NIV" and "New International Version" are trademarks registered in the United States Patent and Trademark Office by Biblica, Inc.™ | Scripture quotations marked NKJV are taken from the New King James Version®. Copyright © 1982 by Thomas Nelson. Used by permission. All rights reserved. | Scripture quotations marked NLT are taken from the Holy Bible, New Living Translation, copyright © 1996, 2004, 2015 by Tyndale House Foundation. Used by permission of Tyndale House Publishers, Inc., Carol Stream, Illinois 60188. All rights reserved. | Scriptures marked TNIV taken from the Holy Bible, New International Reader's Version®. NIrV®. Copyright © 1994, 1996 by International Bible Society. Used by permission of Zondervan. All rights reserved.

For foreign and subsidiary rights, contact the author.

Cover design by: Joe DeLeon

ISBN: 978-1-950718-88-7   1 2 3 4 5 6 7 8 9 10

Printed in the United States of America

LIVING AT THE NEXT

LEADERS EDITION

LEVEL

COURTNEY MCBATH

AVAIL

CONTENTS

FOREWORD

I remember the first time I sat down and talked with Courtney McBath. I had just arrived in Norfolk, Virginia, where I was scheduled to speak at his conference. More than once, I had heard others extol him as a "new voice"—a leader I needed to meet—and when I did meet with Courtney, I found a man who surpassed the praise.

Courtney McBath is a sleeping giant—a leader whose voice, I believe, could be of international consequence. His love for God, his family, and his church has inspired many in the faith, and he has built an organization that is impacting his generation. What particularly struck me on first meeting Courtney is that, while he leads a growing church, provides leadership to pastors and ministry leaders around the world, and delivers the Word of God with brilliant oratorical skill, the first thing he wanted to discuss with me was the book he longed to write. I found his passion to communicate through the written word remarkable, and the fruit of that passion you now hold in your hand.

If you have ever been frustrated or dissatisfied in life, then *Living at the Next Level* is for you. In frustration, we often pray big prayers like, "Lord, take me to the 'next level!'" and, "God, I'm ready for my breakthrough!" When nothing extravagant seems to happen in response, our frustration increases, and we become vulnerable to hopelessness—as if God had dropped us and moved on. This book gives us clarity about where we are in the mess of life. God hasn't dropped us. Right in our mess, Courtney explains, when we're living in relationship with God, we are living at the Next Level.

Maybe, like me, you need a book that both reenergizes you in your love for God and provides balanced, practical instruction on how to live in a fulfilling relationship with Him. Maybe you need help seeing your way through the frustration and pain of difficult life circumstances. Maybe you are looking for a better understanding of godly principles and truths so that you can apply them. *Living at the Next Level*, based on sound teaching from God's Word, answers all of these longings.

Don't you think it's time to stop waiting to get to the Next Level—to stop asking yourself if God will ever take you there and wondering if you're one of the "lucky" Next Level people? Take the advice of my friend, Courtney McBath, and make this powerful request: "Father, teach me how to live at the Next Level and fully experience my friendship journey with You!"

The carefully-crafted text of this book surely sets the ladder against the wall and enables even those who have been challenged by the vicissitudes of life to muster the strength to move from rung to rung. As you scale life's often daunting challenges, know that God is endowing you with the raw courage and naked fortitude you need to elevate your life beyond limitations and reach pinnacles previously unrivaled. This is a good read for the serious soul who, in refusing to come down, often finds him- or herself stranded on the rung of life that leads beyond his or her wildest dreams. If you ever need a shove forward, this is a printed push into a powerful tomorrow. Go ahead—engage and enjoy the journey at the Next Level!

Bishop T.D. Jakes, Sr.
The Potter's House
Dallas, Texas

INTRODUCTION

I can still remember preaching at Trinity Baptist Church in London, England. It was a church comprised of mostly Ghanaians who had relocated to Great Britain. The Lord gave me a message about Peter's imprisonment, and seemingly ensuing death, in Acts 12. After I preached the message, I began preaching the message of Next Level Living everywhere I went. This message was simple: the life you want you already have. Start living at the next level right now! The ultimate in human life is a friendship with an amazing and holy God. How could anything ever top that? Money, fame, influence—nothing comes close to being God's friend—and that is Living at the Next Level.

Today, as I introduce the leader's version of *Living at the Next Level*, I am more convinced than ever of the need to lift up this message. How can we lead people into an intimate and vibrant relationship with God unless we ourselves have that type of relationship? The old proverb is true: "You can't take people where you've never been!" My encouragement to you, ladies and gentlemen, is two-fold.

Determine at the outset that you are going to open your hearts for a renewed passion to walk with God. And resolve that you will experience a change in your leadership influence because you are living under His influence.

Get ready for a wonderful ride into fresh friendship with God, and see the impact it has on your leadership journey.

Courtney McBath, Author
Living at the Next Level, Leaders Edition

PART 1

THE
NEXT
LEVEL
JOURNEY

CHAPTER 1

WHAT IS LIVING AT THE NEXT LEVEL?

My mother looked like a child when she told us. Five feet tall and only thirty years old, she already had youngish looks, but when she made the announcement, something altogether different passed across her face—pure, childlike joy. My little sister and I immediately caught it. None of our friends had done this. We guessed no one in our extended family had even thought to do it. Our parents were always a little ahead of their time—taking us to experience Asian food in our small Tennessee town, inviting a white college student to live with our family for a semester, enrolling us in geeky academic competitions. But this latest plan was in a different league. Disney World had come to the East Coast, and our parents had saved up enough money to take us there during the first summer it was open. We were going to "The Magic Kingdom," the "Wonderful World of Disney"—just like on television!

It was 1972. I was 12 and my sister seven. The Disney budget wasn't expansive enough for flying, so we piled into the camper and drove to Orlando, Florida, from our small town south of Knoxville. The trip would take somewhere around nine hours—enough time for us to ask at least 900 times, "Are we there yet?" We counted Volkswagen Beetles, and my parents listened to Al Green and James Brown. Rest stops, palm trees, gas stations, restaurants, a state that was home to ferocious alligators—if I hadn't known better, I might've begun to believe the road trip was even better than Disney itself.

But, of course, I knew better. Disney was a magical place: a place where dreams came true and everyone became a child again. We had visited amusement parks, but Disney was billed as the ultimate, and it fast became the focal point of all our dreams. Weeks before the trip, my sister and I started planning what we would do once we got there. She imagined being greeted at the gate by Mickey and Donald and having them all to ourselves. I tried to convince her that it wouldn't be just like the television show, but we still stayed up the whole night before we left with visions of what it would be like. The road trip to Orlando might have been exciting, but our dream of Disney was sublime—all wonder and amazement.

Once we began seeing signs for Orlando and Kissimmee, we knew we were getting close. Finally, we pulled into the park. I remember a huge sign with Mickey's picture welcoming us to "Walt Disney World, Home of the Magic Kingdom." Quite simply, we were overwhelmed.

This was it! My sister and I raced from the camper to the shuttle to the gate. Then, I realized that none of what we were about to do was free. Dad had to buy tickets, and at that time, the tickets alone cost him about one-half of his paycheck. But he didn't balk. He paid the price of admission, and they let us in. We had now officially "arrived."

Disney World was magnificent but not exactly what we had imagined. Mickey and Minnie were not standing at the gate to greet us. They didn't go on any rides with us. And, as I recall, it cost money to have lunch with them. You could see them, but you had to go look for them. The rides were a thrill, just as the commercials on television had advertised, but the lines were long, and the sun blistering. From the winding river on the Jungle Cruise to the cool shadows of the Swiss Family Treehouse, we thoroughly enjoyed the adventure; however, bottom line: while Disney was exhilarating, it took some work to get out of it what we had expected.

FRUSTRATION IN THE PLACE OF OUR DREAMS

Looking back on my experience in the Magic Kingdom, I can't help but draw some parallels with the kingdom of God. Like my dad did for us at Disney, Jesus has paid the price for us to get in the gate. Once we accept what Jesus did and choose to enter a relationship, or friendship, with God, we "arrive," having access to experiences of fulfillment that we had only dreamed were possible. The catch is that what we yearn for in life usually doesn't come as quickly, as easily, or packaged as the "commercials" at church might cause us to believe. And that is where frustration, disappointment, and disillusionment can set in. We become confused about how to live and what to expect from life. Constantly striving to get to the place of our dreams, we fail to recognize the truth: We are already there.

Are you seeing long lines at some of the rides you want to take in life? Is the heat of some of your circumstances draining your joy? Do you feel as if you're still waiting for the life you desire to begin? A few years ago, around New Year's, I was wrestling with these issues when I finally hit a wall. I had been asking God to take me to the "next level" in certain areas of my life, but my expectations always seemed to go unmet. Why hadn't I experienced the changes I desired? Why did I feel so stuck? Why wasn't I living the life I really wanted? I had waited. And waited. And I was tired of waiting.

Being a "church boy," I knew all the churchy New Year's Eve clichés: The Battle is WON in 2001. The Lord's gonna bless YOU in 2002. Here comes your VICTORY in 2003. The Lord's gonna give you MORE in 2004. We're coming ALIVE in 2005. Well, almost all of those years had come and gone, and I was still waiting to get to that "next level" where my dreams would finally come true. So, I came up with my own slogan: "This is about to make me SICK in 2006!"

I didn't want to hear anything else about it being "Time for your breakthrough," or, "Your blessing's on the way," or, "This is the year of favor," or, "This is your miracle year," or, "Hold on—you're going to the next level!" I was tired of hearing, and saying, things like, "It's getting ready to happen! Get ready, get ready, get ready!" It seemed I was always getting ready—getting ready to arrive, to go to a new level, to walk into my miracle. "Lord," I said finally, "I want to *live* at the 'next level,' not spend the rest of my life waiting to reach it. Please, just get me there. I want to SEE something!"

You may be feeling that way right now—as if you've been waiting so long for fulfillment in certain areas of life that you can actually feel your hair turning gray. Maybe you're exhausted from propping up your hope only to see it remain just that—a hope. Maybe you've been so hurt or disappointed that you no longer know what or how to pray. If that's you, then hold on. You may be exactly where God wants you. God works with our frustration. Often, He allows our frustration to build and come to a head just so we'll be open to seeing things differently. That's what happened to me.

I wish I'd thought about Disney—about how the long lines and challenges didn't change the fact that I was in the place of my dreams. As I prayed and studied God's Word, it dawned on me that the Next Level was the same. I don't know why I hadn't noticed it before. Once we choose friendship with God, our fulfillment isn't a matter of getting to some new level in life. When we enter that friendship, we *arrive*. Friendship with God *is* the Next Level. Once we "get there," the journey of life in God with all of its ups and downs begins. The ups and downs don't make us any less "there." Consider the Israelites and their arrival in the Promised Land. Once they crossed the Jordan River, they were *in* the land. They still had to explore and take the land; they had some serious battles, enemies, and obstacles in front of them. But once they crossed the Jordan, they were living in the land God had promised them—the place of their dreams, the fulfillment of their destiny.

As God's friends, we too are living in the place of promise. Rather than continuing to exhaust ourselves waiting for or striving to get to some new level—staying discouraged and interpreting struggle as a sign that we haven't yet arrived—we can embrace a different perspective. It's time for a paradigm shift! If we're already at the Next Level, let's quit striving in frustration to get there. Let's dedicate ourselves to learning how to live there: exploring, growing, and journeying in friendship with God.

FULFILLMENT ON THE PATH OF LIFE

Frustration over unmet expectations can produce a few different responses. One is to give up on your dreams. Maybe, in your frustration, you start to feel as if God doesn't see you, doesn't really love you, doesn't have plans or a purpose for you. You wonder if God even wants to move things ahead in your life—if He even cares.

What's more, you begin to think, maybe He *can't* move things ahead for you. You begin to doubt not just His love but also His supernatural power. Finally, you say in your heart, *Well, I guess it's never going to happen. I might as well back off and let my dream die.*

Another response to frustration is to grit your teeth, swallow your pain, and go back to that "waiting-to-arrive" posture. "Maybe next year it will happen," you tell yourself. "Maybe the year after that. Maybe after I get married." You continue to bear up under disappointment when things don't work out as you'd hoped, dreamed, or planned. You put your faith back in the language of those clichéd New Year's promises and cover your doubts, fears, and hurts with misplaced hope. Waiting on life to happen, you go on missing out on *life*; fixated on the destination, you miss the journey.

This book presents a third response to the frustrations of life: learn to fully experience your journey with God right now. Journeying in friendship with God is what living at the Next Level is all about. By taking your mind off of getting to some new level in the future and learning to live at the real Next Level now, you will discover, first, that you don't have to give up on your dreams. Delay doesn't mean denial. God does have plans for you to "see something." He wants you to experience the dreams and desires that He has placed in your heart. As you keep walking in friendship with Him, embracing the journey as it unfolds, you will come into His plans for you in the right way at the right time.

Additionally, you will find that you don't have to burn up your energy anticipating some mysterious future moment when your breakthrough will come and all your dreams will be realized. You can experience your breakthrough right now as you learn to walk with God; everything you need and long for can be found in Him! This is how we transform our life's frustrations into fulfillment: as we enjoy God, explore the Next Level, and discover the life that He has planned for us, we learn that there is something *even better* than what we were trying to achieve—and *that* is simply living in love with God.

In the Psalms, David writes, "You will make known to me the path of life; in Your presence is fullness of joy; in Your right hand there are pleasures forever" (Psalm 16:11, NASB). In the Bible, the "right hand" is a symbol of friendship. Experiencing the unpredictable, sometimes arduous, sometimes exhilarating, path of life in our Friend's presence—not at some future time, but right now—is what brings ultimate fulfillment.

UNDERSTANDING THE JOURNEY

Throughout this book, we will be tracking with a man named Peter over a stretch of his life's journey. The apostle Peter was Jesus' right-hand man, appointed as a key leader of the early church, which exploded on the scene in Jerusalem at Pentecost, nearly two months after Jesus' ascension into heaven. A dozen or so years later, Herod cracked down on the church, killed the apostle James, and threw Peter in prison, slapping him with a trial date—which was basically as good as a death sentence. While Peter sat chained between two guards in a prison, awaiting his fate, the believers whom he led prayed for his safety night and day.

As we will see, God's plans for Peter differed from Herod's. In a dramatic prison break, Peter was escorted out of his cell by an angel of the Lord, led back into the city of Jerusalem, and set free. But even while he was sitting chained in prison, uncertain whether he would live or die, Peter was living at the Next Level. He was still God's friend, God's chosen leader. Someone could have looked at Peter and said, "Man, that guy must've really messed up. He can't be a friend of God." But Peter was an intimate friend of God. Right there in the most con-straining place he could've landed—a prison—Peter was on the path of life, journeying in friendship with God.

While we follow Peter, we will grow in our understanding of God's ways, our friendship with Him, and the phases, twists, and turns of our own paths. We will see that, even while our journeys may include times of limitation or immobility, we are still very much in motion. Even in "prison," we are growing, making progress, walking with God on the path of life, and just as capable of experiencing joy, peace, and fulfillment as at any other point. Prison was merely a phase of Peter's journey, and our current limitations represent only one aspect of the whole of ours. One's journey with God includes a wide variety of terrains and experiences: highs and lows, mountains and valleys, struggles and rest periods, times of fatigue and exhilaration. God uses all of these to draw us to Himself and to fulfill the purpose and plans for which He made us.

As we spend time learning more about the journey, we will need to maintain certain heart attitudes in order to keep from falling back into old patterns of thinking. Keep these attitudes at the forefront of your heart:

1. A heart for friendship with God
2. A heart of gratitude to God
3. A heart of expectancy toward God
4. A heart to seek God

In different phases of our journey, some of these heart attitudes may stand out more prominently than others, but all operate together to keep us on the path God prepared for us before we were born. God told the prophet Jeremiah, "Before I formed you in the womb I knew you" (Jeremiah 1:5, NIV). God knows us and, as He later prophesied through Jeremiah, He knows the plans that He has for us—plans to give us "a future and a hope" (Jeremiah 29:11, NKJV). Maintaining healthy heart attitudes based on God's truth will help us walk in those plans—for, just as in any physical journey, the condition of a person's heart determines his or her level of endurance.

Next Level Heart Attitudes
1. A Heart for Friendship with God
2. A Heart of Gratitude to God
3. A Heart of Expectancy Toward God
4. A Heart to Seek God

PACKING UP OUR TENTS

A lot hangs on our choice to embrace our journey with God and learn to live at the Next Level. If we stick with our old "waiting-to-get-there" mindset, not only will we stay exhausted with frustration, but we will also play right into our enemy's hand. Satan's goal is to keep us believing we haven't arrived. He knows that, if we see the truth about where we are in God, our actions and life choices will change. We will—today—begin taking the land and seizing the opportunities in front of us.

If I had refused to believe I was at Disney World just because I hadn't seen Mickey or Minnie, I might've lingered just inside the gate, wondering when I was going to get to the *real* Disney. Meanwhile, I would have missed the experience of the park altogether. If the Israelites, once they had crossed the Jordan, had refused to believe they were in the land just because they were still camping in tents, they might've stayed in one spot and never gotten up to take the cities God had promised to give them (Deuteronomy 6:10-12).

The same scenario could happen to you. If you get stuck waiting on life at some new level to begin, you might settle for tents and miss the experience of your cities. But once you realize that, as God's friend, you've already reached the Next Level, you will move out into life and put your faith in the God of Right Now. You'll say, "Lord, I may not be seeing all of my dreams come to pass yet, but I know where I am; I refuse to let the enemy get me off the path of life. I won't turn back. I won't stop. I'm going to enjoy our friendship and keep on walking until I experience all that You have for me. Waiting to get there is over. I'm at the Next Level right now, and I'm ready to learn how to live here!"

The enemy hates that kind of faith and determination. He hates your decision to embrace your journey with God. But I thank God the enemy is already defeated, and we serve a God who had plans for us before we were conceived. God wants to reveal His plans and teach us how to journey with Him, so let's make a choice. Let's entrust our issues and irritations to Him, pack up these tents, and move out into life. An incredible adventure awaits us if we'll just get moving. Let's discover what's out there at the Next Level. Are you ready? Will you make the decision? We can start our search where it really begins—by learning what it means to be friends with God.

Mapping Your Next Level Leadership Journey

At the close of each chapter, I want to give you some encouragement and next steps based on the truth you've encountered in it. Please write in this book, and use a journal to extract as much as you possibly can from my attempt to add value to your leadership journey.

MILE MARKER: WHERE AM I ON THE JOURNEY?

In what areas of your leadership do you feel the most frustrated?

_____

_____

_____

What's your "Disney World"—the place that's not quite as good as you expected?

_____

_____

_____

What causes you to struggle to believe that God can use you to lead at higher levels?

_____

_____

_____

Do you have dreams that you've given up on?

_____

_____

_____

Have you become so fixated on the future that, at times, you fail to acknowledge what has already been given to you?

_____

_____

_____

CHARTING YOUR COURSE:
FOCUSING ON THE PATH AHEAD

Now that you have identified some areas of frustratio—and even disappointment—you can move beyond them. Your leadership need not be distracted by unfulfilled expectations. Embrace the leadership opportunities you have now, and allow today's successes to change tomorrow's trajectory.

What steps can you take to refocus on your present and current leadership responsibilities? List 3-4 next steps.

1._____

_____

2._____

_____

3._____

_____

4._____

_____

LEADER'S PRAYER: ASKING FOR GUIDANCE

"Father, thank You for the opportunities You have given me to serve others and to enhance lives. I don't take for granted any of the influence You have given me. Today, I let go of my frustrations about what hasn't happened yet, and set my heart to fully embrace what I have. Give me a spirit of excellence, and let my success today be the change factor for my tomorrow. In Jesus' name, amen."

LEADER'S WORD: RECEIVING
GUIDANCE FROM HIS WORD

"*No, dear brothers and sisters, I have not achieved it, but I focus on this one thing: Forgetting the past and looking forward to what lies ahead, I press on to reach the end of the race and receive the heavenly prize for which God, through Christ Jesus, is calling us.*" —*Philippians 3:13-14 (NLT)*

CHAPTER 2

A FRIENDSHIP JOURNEY: WHAT WE WERE MADE FOR

I only remember a few of the details: it was Sunday morning, August 1968. I don't recall whether the day was bright or overcast, though it must not have been raining because, afterward, my mother sent me running the one-half mile to my grandmother's house to tell her.

I was dressed in navy blue pants and a white shirt, and I stood in the choir stand, just to the side of the pastor's pulpit, with the other members of the children's choir. Ours was a small brick church situated on top of a hill near downtown Maryville, Tennessee, in the foothills of the Great Smoky Mountains.

Our little church of about 100 people drew folk from as far away as Knoxville—about 15 miles—and as close as walking distance. My parents, sister, and I drove in from another small town about 20 minutes away. I had been in church with my family every week since I could remember. Now, I was eight years old.

As our pastor came to the close of his message, the congregation stood, swaying to the tune of a hymn floating up from the poorly-tuned piano. Then, as he did every time he preached, our pastor gave an invitation to receive Christ. What I remember distinctly is the decision: I stood up, walked out of the choir stand in front of the church, and told the pastor I wanted to give my heart to the Lord. Someone handed me a handkerchief because I was crying my eyes out. I was the only one who went forward.

Once we got home, my mother sent me right to my grandmother's house next door. When you live in the country, next door can be a long way off. For us, it was one-quarter mile up the hill and one-quarter mile down—but I went running the whole way to tell my grandmother about my decision; and I've been running to tell people about that decision ever since.

When I think back and try to remember how I felt sitting there in the choir stand as the preacher talked, or what prompted me, as an eight-year-old boy, to stand up in front of the congregation and walk forward, crying, to tell the pastor I wanted to accept Jesus as my Savior, I can't really describe it. I don't really know the answer. The only thing I can be sure of is that, on that Sunday morning, I became keenly aware that God wanted me to walk with Him—and in my heart, I longed to do it. This was the beginning of my journey in friendship with God—my arrival at the Next Level.

NEXT LEVEL LIVING BEGINS AND ENDS WITH FRIENDSHIP

The moment you open your heart to receive Christ, you enter a friendship with God and begin your Next Level journey. Friendship with God is the door, the gate, the way in. Jesus said in John 14:6 (ESV), "I am the way, and the truth, and the life." Our friendship with God through Jesus is the way to the path—the beginning of Next Level living. Choosing that friendship is the initiating moment.

Friendship with God is also what sustains us on the journey. It is what gives us the strength to keep going when circumstances change, people vacillate, or the path takes a difficult turn. Through the unpredictable conditions, relationships, and events of life, we find everything we need in God. Joy and pleasure are in His presence, in His right hand, in His friendship (Psalm 16:11). He is our sustaining power.

Finally, our friendship with God is our true destination. Friendship with God is the starting point of the journey, our gateway to the Next Level. Friendship also *is* the Next Level: the place of our dreams and our destiny, the land we're setting out to explore. All the longings of the heart can be discovered in friendship with God. We start in Him, we are sustained in Him, and in Him we are "made complete" (Colossians 2:10). He is the "Alpha and the Omega, the beginning and the end" (Revelation 21:6, KJV).

If we are going to learn how to live at the Next Level, we must cultivate a heart for friendship with God—a heart for God's friendship is our first Next Level heart attitude. Jesus said that, of all the commandments, the greatest is, "And you shall love the Lord your God with all your heart and with all your soul and with all your mind and with all your strength" (Mark 12:30, ESV). Loving God and living in His presence must become our priority, our life's goal, and the "one thing" we desire, as David wrote in the Psalms (Psalm 27:4, KJV). We must give ourselves entirely to walking with God and to staying in love with Him.

Next Level Heart Attitudes
1. A HEART FOR FRIENDSHIP WITH GOD
2. A Heart of Gratitude to God
3. A Heart of Expectancy Toward God
4. A Heart to Seek God

Once we choose God, then we begin the journey of learning to love Him. Does loving God seem daunting or intimidating? It doesn't have to be. David wrote that God would "show [us] the path of life" (Psalm 16:11, NKJV). Loving God is what we were created to do. God made us to live in friendship with Him.

CREATED FOR FRIENDSHIP

In order to discover the purpose of something, you must go back to its origins, its beginnings. When we go to Scripture and consider the creation of humanity, God's purpose in making us becomes clear. From the very beginning, God wanted friends. That is what our history is about—God pursuing people to be His friends.

Some people believe that God reaches out to us and saves us just so we can spend eternity in heaven. I'm excited to spend eternity in heaven. I'm grateful I've been saved from spending it somewhere else. But God doesn't extend His friendship just to keep us out of hell. Jesus came so that we could live in friendship with God and walk closely with Him on earth.

The book of Revelation teaches us that everything was created for God's pleasure. In a picture of worship around God's throne, 24 elders bow down, declaring to God, "For thou hast created all things, and for thy pleasure they are and were created" (Revelation 4:11, KJV). Everything was created, as another translation says, because God "wanted it" (NCV).

I want you to catch this. God gets pleasure from His creation. In the creation account in Genesis, God said, "Let there be light," and then He "saw that the light was good" (Genesis 1:3-4, NIV). Likewise, when He created the oceans and the dry land, God saw that it was good. Flowers bloom, are pollinated, and produce seed and fruit because that pleases God. Flowers and plants take in carbon dioxide and release oxygen, which we breathe in, and God says, "Oh, that pleases me!" Birds migrate, lions hunt, the sun warms the earth, and the planets stay in their orbits, all because those things please God. He created everything for His pleasure.

Now consider this: if the whole of creation pleases God—if the things He spoke into existence, as Genesis tells us, please Him—then how much more is He pleased by the person He fashioned with His eternal hands out of the ground, the very dust? How much more does God want us, the crown of His creation, into whom He "breathed … the breath of life," to please Him (Genesis 2:7, NIV)? I'm not talking about pleasing Him by doing everything right all the time—although we do try to do right—but rather, pleasing Him by loving Him, by walking closely with Him in friendship, as we were made to do.

When God made Adam, He said, "Let Us make man in Our image, according to Our likeness" (Genesis 1:26, NASB). Adam was the only creature in the garden made in the image of God—with a conscience, a spirit. Adam walked and talked with God in the cool of the day. God loved him, instructed him, and revealed His secrets to him. Adam cared for the earth. He operated in authority and dominion. He knew how to do this because he lived in friendship with God. And that is what made the Garden of Eden a paradise: everything fulfilled its purpose as God had created it. "Behold," we read of God's response as He surveyed creation the day He made Adam, "it was very good" (Genesis 1:31, ESV).

Then God said of Adam, "It is not good for the man to be alone" (Genesis 2:18, NIV). Think about this for a moment. Adam didn't know that he was alone. He didn't go to God and say, "I'm alone. I need a wife, a friend." He couldn't come up with that by himself. He was walking with God, tending the plants, naming the animals—he had no idea he was alone. So what drove God to address this issue of Adam's being alone? I believe God was identifying with Adam. "Adam," I can hear God saying, "I know what it's like having no one on earth you can really connect with. Giraffes can't connect with you; leopards can't do it; orangutans can't do it. They don't have enough in common with you. You need someone who can choose to be your friend. As God, I am complete in myself, and I have angels and the heavenly hosts around me; however, I still want to connect with someone who is made in my image, who shares things in common with me, and who can choose to be my friend."

My own take is that, once Adam met Eve, he finally got it. He realized that he had been alone—big time.

THE FIGHT

We're going to stay in the garden a little longer, because I want you to see something about the power of purpose. Immediately when we lock into our primary, God-given purpose—friendship with God—we draw fire from the enemy. We become a target. Or more specifically, our purpose—that friendship—becomes a target. That's exactly what happened with Adam and Eve. They were living at the Next Level, enjoying friendship with God in the garden, when the serpent, the devil, showed up.

Let's consider the background. We'll begin with an angel named Lucifer.

In the book of Isaiah, we find a figurative picture of a heavenly battle that some scholars believe took place before the creation of humanity. Here's the setup: on one side, you have God, Creator and Ruler of heaven and earth, and on the other side, an archangel, Lucifer, who some theologians believe was in charge of musical worship in the heavens. Passages in Isaiah and Ezekiel could be translated as describing this angel having "stringed instruments" (Isaiah 14:11, NKJV) and "timbrels and pipes" (Ezekiel 28:13, NKJV).

If he led worship, as some believe, then Lucifer was given a high calling and position. "You had the seal of perfection," the Bible says, "Full of wisdom and perfect in beauty …. Every precious stone was your covering …. You were the anointed cherub who covers, and I [the Lord] placed you there. You were on the holy mountain of God" (Ezekiel 28:12-14, NASB).

So Lucifer was at the top of his game. He was present on the mountain of God, by some accounts leading worship; but he decided that wasn't enough. He wanted the things reserved only for God—the glory, worship, and praise. Hence, the battle. As the fight ensued, Lucifer declared, "I will ascend to heaven; I will raise my throne above the stars of God …. I will make myself like the Most High" (Isaiah 14:13-14, NASB).

That was quite a declaration. Of course, as would anyone battling with God, Lucifer lost. I can imagine God saying, "You'd better think about that again," and promptly casting Lucifer out, banishing him from the holy mountain. At this point, for Lucifer, at least two things were true: he was angry, and he was ready to take out his wrath on whomever he could find.

Enter Adam.

Lucifer, also known as Satan, immediately had issues with Adam. I can picture Satan, the angel perhaps once in charge of the intimate act of worship in heaven, now running into this new earthly inhabitant with a wonderful, intimate friendship with the same God who had just kicked him, Satan, out. To add insult to injury, Satan discovered that God actually said of Adam, "I'm going to create him in my image." So while Satan was kicked out of heaven for trying to be like God, Adam received an invitation to take on God's character—no, worse: God made Adam in His image.

Since Satan couldn't fight God, he went after the next in line: the guy made in the image of God. Remember, Adam had two things on Satan. He was created to be what Satan could not be—like God. And he had an intimate friendship with God, as Satan once had possessed but had lost. In short, Satan's new mission was to somehow stop Adam and his wife, Eve, from having what he could no longer have. It's the classic quarrel: "If I can't have Him, then nobody can."

Keep in mind that Satan is crafty, and his tactics in the garden had been shrewdly conceived. He knew God wouldn't forsake His friends, so he devised a plan to entice God's friends to forsake Him. After all, Adam and Eve had free will; they could choose. And since God had only one primary commandment—regarding the Tree of Knowledge of Good and Evil: "Don't eat of it; that's part of My covenant with you"—the devil focused on the one thing Adam and Eve had to do—or, rather, *not* do—to maintain their fellowship with God.

The point was to tempt Adam and Eve into separating themselves from God and operating independently of Him. Satan wanted them thinking this way: *We've got the knowledge now. Now that we've eaten the fruit, we've got all that we need without having to meet with God every afternoon. There's no need to take all that trouble. We can do this ourselves.*

And, as we know, that is exactly what happened.

YOUR FIGHT

Fast-forward to your life today. As with Adam and Eve in the garden, every temptation you face—every battle you fight—on your Next Level journey is ultimately about one thing: your primary purpose of being God's friend.

If you believe the devil exists and is real, and that you are his enemy, then take heed: know that he is aiming to destroy the very purpose for which you were made: real, intimate friendship with God. This is not your classic Flip Wilson, "The devil made me do it" speech. I don't believe the devil is behind every adverse circumstance we face. But when the devil actually interferes with your life, be assured that he's after your purpose—that friendship. He's jealous of the position and influence you have with God.

Have you ever thought to yourself, *It seems like every time I start getting close to God, "all hell breaks loose"?* I'm not using the expression about hell profanely—I mean it literally. Why would things seem to go haywire the minute you make a move to get closer to God? Because the one who controls hell doesn't want you to be close to God! When you start to move in close, the enemy starts rattling. You see, when you're distant from God, you're not a threat. You don't disturb the devil. He doesn't even mind if you're a church member. But the minute you move toward God, everything changes. The devil hates those who want to be intimate friends with God. Satan doesn't want to see you in his former place.

On the other hand, some of the battles and limitations in your life can't be blamed on the devil. Some things that happen in life are just that—life. Jesus said, "In this world you will have trouble" (John 16:33, TNIV). Maybe you're dealing with frustration in some of your relationships, disappointment over missed opportunities, the pain of unexpected loss, or discouragement about where you are spiritually. These challenges aren't necessarily caused by the devil. They are, however, related to your friendship with God. All of our challenges have the potential to affect that friendship—to build it up or tear it down.

Consider for a moment, too, that God Himself might be the one stirring things up in your life. What you think is the devil's doing or life happening might actually be God fighting for your friendship. God doesn't want to be replaced by your relationships, your dreams, or your professional ambitions. God made you to be His friend and, if something is threatening your love for Him, He will insert Himself to get your attention. God, not the devil, may be the one rattling your cage. Consider as you pray that God may be the one invading your life because He's after your heart.

THE RESTORER

If we're going to connect the dots between Satan's fall from heaven, the fall of humanity, and the limitations and struggles you're facing right now on your Next Level journey, all we need to do is open the Bible. The Bible is an account of God's constant, vigilant work to bring us back into friendship with Himself.

I love what God tells Moses in Exodus 19. God has delivered Israel from slavery in Egypt and, by a miracle, has taken the people across the Red Sea. Now, He instructs Moses to tell the people, "I bore you on eagles' wings, and brought you to Myself [to be My own possession]" (Exodus 19:4-5, ESV).

God is a jealous God. The first of the Ten Commandments He gives the people through Moses is, "You shall have no other gods before Me" (Deuteronomy 5:7, NIV). God didn't say, "Don't worship other gods because it's bad for your health. Don't worship them because they'll do you wrong. Don't worship them because they'll mess up my plans for your life." God said, "Tell the people not to worship other gods because I'm a jealous God. I'm serious about My place in their lives. I am God. I brought them to myself. They belong to Me. And I want to be the center of their attention" (Deuteronomy 5:9, author's paraphrase).

Throughout the Bible, we see God raising up prophets and deliverers to rescue His people and put them back on track, in relationship with Him. We read about judges like Deborah, Gideon, and Samson; kings like Saul, David, and Solomon; prophets like Elijah, Isaiah, and Jeremiah; and leaders like Ezra, Nehemiah, and Zerubbabel. God sent these men and women to restore the people to Himself. Then, after the prophet Malachi, for about 400 years, the Bible is silent—until the Ultimate Restorer arrives.

Enter the God-man: Jesus.

The Bible says, "The Son of God appeared for this purpose, to destroy the works of the devil" (1 John 3:8, NASB). What is the work of the devil? We've just seen it: the work of the devil is to separate humanity from God. Maybe you thought the work of the devil was crack cocaine. Maybe you thought it was murder, abuse, embezzlement, or pornography. The devil is certainly at work in these things, but they are only signs of his ultimate work, which is to cut off our friendship with God. When we are disconnected from God, we more readily yield to decisions and behaviors that bring destruction in our lives and in the lives of others. But if we can commit to staying connected to God, He will help us stay on the path of life, and will even make the fallout from our sin eventually work for our good (Romans 8:28).

So how did Jesus destroy the devil's work and restore us to friendship with God? Let's go back to the garden. As in any friendship, when a contract is broken—when someone doesn't keep his or her end of a bargain—the relationship is impeded. So it was with Adam and Eve. They broke covenant with God. They ate fruit from the one tree God told them not to eat of, and they lost the privilege of intimacy with Him. Just as Satan was thrown off the mountain of God, so Adam and Eve were cast out of the garden. The devil, of course, believed he had succeeded. "If I can't have Him, nobody will" seemed to have worked. He thought it was over for Adam, Eve, and the rest of us made in God's image. "They've committed high treason. Now they'll never get back," was Satan's perspective on the fall.

But doesn't the devil know it yet? Whenever God closes a door, He opens a window. God makes a way when there seems to be no way. That's why Jesus said, "I am the way, and the truth, and the life" (John 14:6, NASB). He was saying, "I am the way back to friendship with

God. I am the truth about friendship with God. I am Life for you, because friendship with God *is* your life."

JOINED BACK TOGETHER

Jesus' ability to restore us to friendship with God was based on a couple of things. First, He was both God and man. He was sinless and perfect; He was holy, and His blood was holy. However, at the same time, He came in a man's body, so He could relate to people's faults and issues. He understood us completely. Without sinning, He was tempted just as we are (Hebrews 4:15).

Secondly, Jesus loved us enough to give His life as a payment for our breach of contract with God. We owed God a debt, and only a perfect sacrifice could be used as a payment. Blood had to be shed, but it had to be blood untainted by Adam's, Eve's, and humanity's rebellion when they disobeyed God (Hebrews 9:22). Jesus, the God-man, was the only one who could do it. By dying for us, He paid off our debt and put us back in a position to negotiate a new contract.

And He didn't stop there. Do you know how contract negotiations can get ugly sometimes? Well, Jesus didn't just die for us. He rose from the dead in order to sit at the right hand of God as our Advocate—our Lawyer—to make sure we could survive the contract negotiations and successfully reconnect with God (1 John 2:1).

The Bible puts it this way: "Therefore, having been justified by faith, we have peace with God through our Lord Jesus Christ" (Romans 5:1, NKJV). "Peace" in this verse doesn't mean the absence of trouble. It doesn't mean the lack of conflict. Peace here is better interpreted as "reconciliation." Once we've placed our faith in what Jesus did to restore us to friendship with God, we experience reconciliation. We have peace with God. The breach is healed. Through Jesus, we have been joined back together with God in friendship.

NO CONDEMNATION

Satan will go to great lengths to keep you from believing that God can forgive you. The Bible calls the devil the "accuser of our brethren" (Revelation 12:10, NKJV). Who are the "brethren"? They are the people of God, the friends of God, men and women who belong to God—you and me. Satan is our accuser, and one of his primary goals is to condemn us.

I've discovered that condemnation is one way the enemy shuts people down. Everyone is going to fail; that's one thing we can count on. Satan counts on it, too—so much so that he has developed a strategy based on our propensity to fall. His strategy is to condemn us into believing that God will never forgive us—that we are separated from God with no way back. But the Bible sets the record straight. Paul wrote, "Therefore, there is now no condemnation for those who are in Christ Jesus" (Romans 8:1, NIV).

In the face of spiritual opposition, we must exercise faith and aggressively take hold of forgiveness. How can we journey in friendship with God if we don't believe that He can really forgive us, accept us, or love us? Maybe you've done something for which you believe God will never forgive you. Maybe you're so torn up over your past sin that you continually ask God for forgiveness—as if He isn't listening, as if asking the first time didn't work. Maybe you're scared because you are struggling with temptation and, in your mind, even being tempted is a sin. It is not, for Jesus was tempted, and He was without sin (Hebrews 4:15).

Let me clear the fear and condemnation out of your heart with the Word of God. The Bible says, "If we confess our sins, He is faithful and righteous to forgive us our sins and to cleanse us from all unrighteousness" (1 John 1:9, ESV). Whatever our sins—whatever—as we come to God with transparent hearts and confess, He will forgive and cleanse, or heal, us. He wants us to know the freedom of a dear heart—a heart set free, both to love Him without distraction and to receive the fullness of His love. That's why He sent Jesus: because He loves us.

MAKING YOUR FRIENDSHIP WITH GOD YOUR PRIORITY

With all of the talk today about breakthroughs and miracles and getting to new levels in life, we so often miss the point. We thought our struggles were about whether we succeeded in achieving some finite set of goals or made enough money to own investment property. We've fought our battles as if they were over externals, and we've kept our eyes on the prizes and rewards of this world. Meanwhile, God has been wooing us, calling to us, and trying to let us know what life's really all about. The Next Level, the journey, the substance of life, and who we are—these are all about walking with God and sharing an intimate friendship with our Creator.

While many of us have entered friendship with God through Jesus Christ, we may not be experiencing a vibrant, intimate relationship with Him. Maybe you simply haven't realized that God wants to be close to you. The Bible calls Abraham "the friend of God," but could God, the Creator, really want the same for us today? Maybe you haven't been able to picture what a friendship with God should look like. Since you haven't known how to enjoy intimacy with God, you've languished, knowing Him only from a distance, experiencing emptiness in your heart and a longing you haven't quite been able to identify.

Because I was young when I gave my heart to God, I was able to begin cultivating my friendship with Him early in life. As an eight-year-old living in a stable home—at least during that time—I didn't have any major distractions, so I could focus on praying and reading God's Word just to get to know Him. Not everyone shares that experience. Whatever your background, the important thing is that you begin prioritizing your friendship with God as soon as possible. Paul wrote that he considered everything in his life to be garbage when compared to loving and being loved by God. "That I may know Him," Paul wrote of Jesus (Philippians 3:10, ESV). *That he may know Him.* That was Paul's heart's desire. Is it yours?

Right now, where you are, you can turn to God in your heart and decide to make knowing Him intimately your life's priority. God wants to be known. Jesus says, "Behold, I stand at the door and knock; if anyone hears My voice and opens the door, I will come in to him and will dine with him, and he with Me" (Revelation 3:20, NASB). Will you open to His love? You can say, "Lord, I'm sorry I've been distant. I understand my purpose better now, and I want to develop a heart for friendship with You. I want to know You intimately. I want to walk with You and experience what it's like to be close. Please teach me and help me."

The Bible promises that, as we draw near to God, He will draw near to us (James 4:8). You've just moved toward God. Now, take a moment to thank God, in faith, for moving toward you. By focusing on our first Next Level heart attitude—a heart for friendship with God—and putting that friendship first, you have set your heart in agreement with God's will for your life. He will move heaven and earth to help you grow in intimacy with Him. He will show you the path of life. He created you to know Him, and He will make Himself known.

GOD'S END OF THE FRIENDSHIP

Even after we decide to make friendship with God our priority, we might continue to struggle with frustration, disappointment, and pain. We still have expectations of life. We still experience crushing blows. We still face battles that cause us to ask, "Isn't this a friendship, God? Why aren't You holding up Your end?"

You may know in your mind that battles come when the enemy attempts to undermine your friendship with God. You may know that limitations are a part of life. You may understand that God even permits certain struggles in life to draw people closer to Him. But knowing these things doesn't necessarily make the struggles easier. When you are walking through pain and can't see the big picture, it takes faith to believe that God can make sense of it and that He still plans to give you "a future and a hope" (Jeremiah 29:11, NASB).

As we are about to learn through Peter's story of imprisonment and release, when we face what appear to be massive obstacles, God is not only closer than ever, but He is also working out His plans for our lives in beautiful, intricate ways. In the heat of battle, God remains our Friend—faithful, involved, and in control. A prison cell door might slam in front of us, but God sees us just as free as ever, and He can open a window. We may feel limited, but through Christ, as Paul wrote, we can do all things (Philippians 4:13). Locked in or locked out, we can fulfill God's plan for our lives and experience the fulfillment of His love right where we are.

Mapping Your Next Level Leadership Journey

MILE MARKER: WHERE AM I ON THE JOURNEY?

You now realize that being a leader is not God's highest priority for you; instead, being His friend is what He wants most. When you lead out of this friendship, it changes the level of effectiveness of your leadership.

What areas of your life distract you from your friendship with God?

_____

_____

_____

What are you battling with that you haven't learned to commit to Him as your Friend?

_____

_____

_____

Knowing you are called to improve others' quality of life, how consistently are you allowing your Friend and Heavenly Father to refresh and renew you?

_____

_____

_____

CHARTING YOUR COURSE: FOCUSING ON THE PATH AHEAD

The first Next Level heart attitude is "A Heart for Friendship with God." Today is a great day to practice following His leadership by asking Him to renew your heart for Him. Ask God what you can do to deepen your friendship with Him. Ask Him to help you make being led by Him a higher priority than leading others.

LEADER'S PRAYER: ASKING FOR GUIDANCE

"Lord, You know I want to be a good leader in the space You have placed me in. But today, I realize that being Your friend is more important than any leadership responsibility. I want to lead people out of the abundance of being friends with You and knowing You well. Help me to make the needed adjustments in my daily activities, thoughts, words, and attitudes so that I can deepen my friendship with You. In Jesus' name, amen."

LEADER'S WORD: RECEIVING GUIDANCE FROM HIS WORD

"'And you must love the Lord your God with all your heart, all your soul, all your mind, and all your strength.'" —Mark 12:30 (NLT)

PART 2

LIMITATIONS AT THE NEXT LEVEL

CHAPTER 3

WHEN THE FRIENDSHIP JOURNEY TAKES AN UNEXPECTED TURN

I've been preaching for more than three decades—since I was 13 years old. Since then, I have seen God move in extraordinary ways; but a few years ago, I experienced one of the strangest seasons of ministry I had known to date. I started preaching about Peter's prison experience and his miraculous release. My foray into the material began in London, England, where I preached to a dynamic congregation of people, many of whom were from Ghana, West Africa.

To several hundred folk packed into an extremely limited physical space, I introduced Peter sitting chained in his prison cell, and then tracked with him as God broke him out of his limitations. The message seemed to explode in that little London building. Many of the people listening had come to England to break out of one set of limitations, only to encounter a whole new set of issues and struggles. Beyond this, the church had long ago outgrown its building. The people were facing the pain of limitations both individually and corporately; and when I began to teach about the work of God in Peter's prison experience, the congregation became intensely focused and engaged. I knew God was up to something...I just didn't know what.

After leaving London, I returned home to our church in Norfolk, Virginia, and soon afterward began traveling to preach in other churches. For several months, as I visited places like Atlanta, Dallas, Raleigh-Durham, and Richmond, I felt compelled to preach the same message about Peter's experience in prison, the way God uses our limitations, and God's ability to bring us out. I don't often preach the same message over and over, but as I would try to prepare different messages for my speaking engagements, I would sense God saying in my heart, *What are you doing? Just keep preaching what I gave you.*

Every time I preached about Peter, the message came out a little differently; but everywhere I went, people responded. They were discovering right along with me that, even in our limitations, we are God's friends, that God uses our struggles to build us, and that, at any moment, God can release us into another phase of our journey. Like the man we are about to meet and follow through the coming chapters, right in our prisons, we are living at the Next Level.

ENTER PETER

Imagine this.

People had gathered from all over the world to celebrate the feast at Jerusalem with dancing, music, and dining. The city center was abuzz with conversation and laughter. There was talk of a new religion that had emerged, only to have its leader—a man named Jesus— executed. About 120 of this man's followers were in the city now and had gathered on the second floor of what some believe was a house. Then, it happened. This diverse group of men and women came stumbling out of the building, down the stairs, and into the street.

Talk immediately picked up: "Can you believe they would be drunk so early in the day? Have they no decency?"

Suddenly, the crowd stopped talking and began to listen. They heard this supposedly drunken lot speaking in various languages about God's wonderful works. No matter where people in the crowd hailed from or what dialect they spoke, all were hearing words about God's love for all people in their own languages.

A buzz of confused whispering arose: "What's going on? Will someone please explain?"

The rabbis scratched their heads. The scribes took copious notes. The Pharisees and Sadducees congregated (separately, of course) to determine who was to blame for this miraculous fiasco.

Then, a scraggly-bearded man stepped onto the makeshift podium and spoke with such power and grace he could've been a scholar at the local graduate school, though everybody knew he was only from that backwoods region of Galilee. His name was Peter. He was the

God-appointed leader of this new sect of Christ-followers, and he eloquently explained the miracle they were observing.

"This," he proclaimed to the crowd, "is the outpouring of God's Spirit upon all people that was promised to us in the prophets."

Unforgettable. Leader of leaders. Well-versed, wise, and articulate. Bold. Unhesitating. Peter.

He would be leading the believers for a long time.

PETER AT THE NEXT LEVEL

Now, let's skip ahead to another scene more than a decade later. By now, Peter had led the followers of Jesus through an astounding period of growth. He and fellow leaders had worked great miracles in Jesus' name, and people in the city were filled with awe. Thousands had joined the new movement, many selling their property to share with the needy. And where the Christ-followers went, they were treated well, finding favor throughout the region.

Then, things changed. A wave of persecution swept the church in Jerusalem, and one of its leaders, Stephen, was publicly stoned. Believers were seized in their homes and dragged off to prison. A huge scattering occurred. The Christ-followers left town in droves, moving their families to places as far away as Asia Minor—and beyond. Peter continued to lead. The movement continued to grow. The authorities continued to crack down. Finally, Herod did what the believers dreaded: he took one of Jesus' 12 apostles—James, the brother of John—and had him killed.

Since many of the city's residents seemed pleased with James' execution, Herod thought he would do one better: he arrested Peter, setting a date for a public hearing and throwing the dwindling community of believers into a state of emergency. As the story opens in Acts 12, we encounter Peter in prison the night before his trial. "Peter was sleeping between two soldiers," we read, "bound with two chains, and guards in front of the door were watching over the prison" (Acts 12:6, NASB).

What must Peter have been thinking in those final hours, as day gave way to night? Perhaps he thought back to that promising day years earlier when, at the feast, he first declared the works of God to people from different nations. Perhaps it crossed his mind that tomorrow he again would stand before the public, this time not as the celebrated leader of the Jesus of Nazareth sect but as a criminal awaiting the sword. Maybe he took heart, trusting that the people he loved and led were praying for him—and they were, day and night. Maybe he still dared to hope. We do know that he was out of options. As night fell, Peter let his head dip between his shoulders and went to sleep.

This image of Peter chained and sleeping between two guards the night before his trial continues to haunt me. How could he do it—sleep? Was he that confident in God, or just exhausted from worry? Had he made up his mind to accept his fate? I can tell you what I would've been thinking: *God, I thought I was your friend, your servant, your appointed leader. Why did you change your mind about me? I thought I was supposed to take care of your people. Is it over already?*

Peter, it appeared, would never become what he anticipated. Once impetuous and spontaneous, sometimes exhibiting spurts of greatness and—at other times, failed judgment—the former fisherman had risen to the demands of his day and served the people faithfully, only to see his life seemingly coming to an abrupt end. Tomorrow, he would be gone. Promises and plans wouldn't matter. Peter would be history. Or so it seemed.

But hadn't Peter heard it from Jesus himself: "With God all things are possible" (Matthew 19:26, NIV)? What looked one way to Herod, the guards and, perhaps, even to Peter looked different to God. He had already determined there would be no trial, no execution, no appointment with the sword for Peter. Peter's prison was about to be transformed from a place of finality into a springboard for spectacular beginnings. Hardly the end of the road, the prison was the starting point for another leg of Peter's Next Level journey. God was about to give Peter a firsthand lesson in removing limitations.

PRISON ON THE FRIENDSHIP JOURNEY

When our journey in friendship with God seems to lead us to prison, we have to process our way through a storm of emotions. "What happened?" we want to know. There we were—we made ourselves vulnerable to God. We committed to being His friend. We opened our hearts to Him. We asked Him to help us learn to love Him better. We were doing our part, cultivating that first Next Level heart attitude—a heart for His friendship—and now, suddenly, we find ourselves arrested, thrown into a cell, locked down in chains, and slapped with a trial date. We don't see our prison as a "springboard for spectacular beginnings." We wonder if we will ever fulfill the dreams and plans in our hearts.

With our heads spinning, we ask God what Peter and the disciples once asked Jesus when they were crossing the Sea of Galilee in a storm. Jesus was asleep in the stern. The boat was filling up. Finally, the disciples woke Him and said, "Teacher, don't you care if we drown?" (Mark 4:38, TNIV). Chained between two guards in our cell, we ask the same thing: "God, don't you care?"

When I was 13 years old, I found myself in this very position. There I was, walking in friendship with God—getting to know Him, even involved in ministry and leading others to Christ at a young age—when suddenly, the life I had known was snatched away from me. My mom and dad began arguing. Our home became filled with confusion and anger and, not long after that trip to Disney World, my parents separated and later divorced. My security was gone. My daily life was unrecognizable. The dreams in my heart came to seem more like pipe dreams than possibilities.

How had this happened? I had grown up in a kid's fantasy world: nice house, family vacations, involved parents, two sets of grandparents, and even a great-grandmother. All my life, my parents had been connected at the hip. They built our house when I was a small child, and I can still remember, after the faucets were first installed in one of the bathrooms, my dad rushing in to the kitchen, exclaiming, "Connie, the handles on the faucets have our initials on them! *H* and *C* for Herman and Connie." Now, as a young teenager, I was two steps away from the poverty level, living in a single-parent home we shared with my grandmother. How did I get from life in a happy family to a place I call Child-of-Divorce Prison? If I were God's friend, then why was I in this position? Didn't He care?

As we follow Peter, we'll learn more about the ways God works in our personal prisons, using the very things that hurt us and hold us down to make us the people He intends us to be. I experienced this redemptive work myself when, at 13, in the midst of my own upheaval and pain, I was given many opportunities to do what I longed to do—preach. There I was, wrestling with my chains, when God awakened my gift. Right there in the prison, my life's calling was born.

Does God care when your journey lands you in prison? Let's look at how Jesus responded when the disciples, faced with having to bail water out of their boat during the storm, asked Him if He cared about their fate. Not wasting any breath, Jesus got up, calmed the storm, and then asked, "Why are you afraid? Do you still have no faith?" (Mark 4:40, NASB) His response sounds cutting, but Jesus wasn't condemning the disciples. He was highlighting an unshakable truth: God is our Friend. His love and faithfulness are fixed, unwavering. He never leaves us. He can change things in a moment. If we've landed in a prison, God knows why and has plans to work our incarceration out for our good. He is keeping us on the path of life, even when it feels like we've been hurled headlong into a ditch.

YOUR LIMITATIONS

Years after his prison experience, Peter wrote, "Dear friends, do not be surprised at the fiery ordeal that has come on you to test you, as though something strange were happening to you" (1 Peter 4:12-13, TNIV). *Do not be surprised.* Peter was writing about specific kinds of trials and limitations—those that come as the results of one's commitment to Christ. Remember, Peter was leading a church in crisis—a persecuted, scattered church. He was simply restating what Jesus had once told him: "'Servants are not greater than their master.' If they persecuted me, they will persecute you also" (John 15:20, TNIV).

While we may suffer as a direct result of our friendship with God, we can also wind up in prison for other reasons. Hindrances are an integral part of our Next Level journey. We may feel devastated by them when they come but, in some regard, we shouldn't be surprised by them, as if "something strange" were happening. Jesus said, "In this world you will have trouble" (John 16:33 TNIV). Let's look at some of the types of limitations we'll face in life.

Limitations You Can't Control

Some of your limitations may be the result of the actions, or inactions, of others. In other words, they may be caused by factors you can't control.

Maybe you feel limited by the circumstances into which you were born. You may see your country of origin as a limitation. Maybe your parents didn't place a high premium on education, and you believe their failure to prioritize it now leaves you at a disadvantage. Maybe your parents left you to be reared by someone else. Maybe they were addicted to drugs. Maybe you suffered abuse or neglect. You find yourself wondering, *Why did I come into this world with so many cards stacked against me—with so many obstacles that other people don't seem to have to overcome?*

I have felt the same way. I couldn't control being born in the rural American South at the end of the 1950s, when African Americans were suffering great oppression. I was devastated as an adolescent by the breakup of my family. Peter must have felt pretty limited as he tried to lead a global movement, having grown up in the remote region of Galilee with fishing as his only vocational training. What you may feel about your situation makes sense in human terms, and it makes sense to God. He knows just where you are. "You understand my thought from afar," David wrote of God in Psalm 139:2 (NASB). But more than understanding us, God also has a plan to utilize the cards we've been dealt—the cards He knew we would be dealt—for His redemptive purposes.

Sometimes, those purposes require us to take action. Being born into a family in which nobody has a college education, for instance, doesn't stop you from signing up for classes. Growing up in a family with three generations of divorce doesn't prevent you from being purposeful about succeeding in your own marriage. Maybe you experienced trauma or abuse as a child and need to consider the process of counseling. The point is that, while you may not be able to alter your family of origin, make other people change, or undo the painful events of the past, at least you can take a stand for your own future and for the generations that will follow you. From this perspective, the limitations you can't change or control actually can become your motivation to choose a different course for your life!

Limitations That Result from Your Own Actions or Decisions

It is one thing to believe God will see us through limitations created by others, or through situations over which we have no control; but what about limitations caused by decisions we ourselves have made? What about those times when we had absolute control and, whether we sinned or simply acted unwisely, we simply did the wrong thing?

Maybe you left college two years into your degree when you should've stayed and completed it. Maybe you made an unwise job change. Maybe you ignored a host of red flags and jumped into a romantic relationship that ended in trouble. Maybe you initiated a divorce for reasons you now question. What do we do about these kinds of limitations? Why would God want to bring us relief when we have caused these limitations ourselves?

First, if your limitations are the result of sin on your part, remember that God can forgive you. Because Jesus gave Himself to restore us to friendship with God, you have the right to go to God in prayer, tell Him about your sin, and ask for His forgiveness. This is a critical way that you maintain your friendship connection with God. When you go to Him with your sin, God promises not just to forgive you but also to heal you of the issues and motivations that drive you to sin in the first place (1 John 1:9).

Even beyond forgiving you and dealing with your sin issues, God can take a past sin—or, if not a sin, an unwise decision—work with it, and *still* perform His will in your life. Yes, we have to face the consequences of our actions; we must accept that we often bring repercussions and limitations onto ourselves. But God can turn our circumstances around and compensate for our past mistakes, bad judgments, and sins. He loves us. In whatever way He pleases, He can remove or mitigate our self-generated limitations.

Consider the Old Testament prophet Jonah. He really created some limitations for himself. God said, "Go to Nineveh," and Jonah—on purpose—boarded a ship that took him in the opposite direction. The result? Jonah got thrown overboard and swallowed by a fish—and you can bet he endured some pretty unsavory "prison" conditions. But notice the way the story changed course: once Jonah's heart turned back to God, the fish spit him out onshore. It was as if God said, "Jonah, let's try this again. And I want you to get it right this time!"

That same Jonah scenario can play out in our lives. We may sin or make wrong decisions—even unintentionally—and, as a result, we may spend a little time underwater. But when we turn our hearts to God, He has a remarkable way of making up for lost time and direction—for getting us right back where we should've been, could've been, and would've been if we had just done the right thing starting out. Amazingly, He can give us chance after chance to start over and "get it right this time."

What about those decisions that can't be reversed or undone? We may not get another chance to go to Nineveh as Jonah did—we may not get back exactly what we lost. But the heart of redemption is that, even in the midst of our mess, God still has plans for our lives. However He chooses to make up for what we forfeited or lost, ultimately, He will make our lives fruitful again. That is the promise to which we must cling.

Limitations That Result from Life Happening

Trouble comes—Jesus said it. Some of our limitations are simply the result of things that go on in life: the loss of a job, the loss of a loved one, a physical challenge, or even a natural disaster. Some events and circumstances we cannot explain, so I want to make a profound theological statement—a complex, bold assertion—and here it is: *stuff happens.*

So often, when we encounter difficulty, we wear ourselves out trying to pinpoint the cause and determine where we are responsible—or where others are responsible. Jesus said we would have trouble in life! Some things just happen. Stop looking for where to place blame. Stop trying to figure it all out, wondering what you might have done to bring it on yourself. Not every difficulty comes into our lives by way of people's failings—including ours—and we can become debilitated when we overanalyze our circumstances.

The beautiful thing about God is that even the limitations that come with living on earth do not limit what He wants to do in our lives. Remember His promise: "'For I know the plans that I have for you … plans for welfare and not for calamity to give you a future and a hope'" (Jeremiah 29:11, NASB). We may not know the plans, but God says He knows the plans He has for us. That truth alone can be a great comfort. No matter what we believe or see happening around us, God loves us, He knows what He's doing, and He says His plans for us are good.

TRUSTING GOD IN LIMITATIONS

Now comes the difficult part. We may have gained insight into the nature of some of our limitations and a greater awareness of God's presence with us in them. We may recognize that God remains our Friend in difficulty, and that He hasn't betrayed us just because we've landed in a prison. Even so, we still have to trust Him to mend our hearts, redeem our confines, and help us live in peace as long as they last. We need God's help. We can't walk this leg of the journey in our own strength. If our strength and determination were enough, then we would've already surmounted our obstacles. At a certain point, we must engage our faith, as Jesus told the disciples in that boat, and trust our Friend to do the deep work that only He can do.

One of the ways we develop an ability to trust God in the midst of limitations is by expressing thanks for the ways He has addressed them in the past. A heart of gratitude to God is the second Next Level heart attitude we need to cultivate as we journey with Him. Gratitude honors God, and it sustains us in trouble, allowing us to release our frustrations and rest. By giving God thanks, we actively remember what He has done already to bring us healing and change; in rehearsing those memories back to Him, we build up an ability to trust Him now. God constantly instructed the Israelites to build altars as reminders of His faithfulness. The first thing the people did after they traversed the Jordan River's dry riverbed, where they had miraculously crossed to enter the Promised Land, was set up a memorial of stones (Joshua 4:1-7; 20-24). Gratitude for God's faithfulness is the starting point of trust.

Next Level Heart Attitudes
1. A Heart for Friendship with God
2. A HEART OF GRATITUDE TO GOD
3. A Heart of Expectancy Toward God
4. A Heart to Seek God

Think about it: you know in your heart that you're not where you used to be. You may be experiencing hardship, but there was a time when you were in a down place, a low place—as David wrote, a "horrible pit"—and God brought you out (Psalm 40:2, NKJV). Take a moment to remember that experience and say, "Lord, I may be in the middle of this current limitation, but I rejoice and thank You that I'm not where I used to be!"

Now that you've thanked God for His faithfulness in the past, you can more confidently thank Him for the work He chooses to do in the future. In faith, you can say, "Even though I don't see it yet, Lord, I believe that you are working in my situation. You were faithful before, so I trust you now, and I thank you for what I don't yet see." Do you see how gratitude can be an expression of trust?

Notice, too, how giving thanks deepens friendship with God, building us up in our first Next Level heart attitude: a heart for His friendship. In fact, the entry point into God's presence is gratitude. The psalmist wrote, "Enter His gates with thanksgiving and His courts with praise" (Psalm 100:4, BSB). By "thanksgiving" we approach God. As we express our gratitude, we are loving Him. And whatever we may be dealing with, whatever may go our way or not go our way in life, loving God is never a waste of our time. The closer we get to Him, the sweeter and more fulfilling the path of life becomes, whether we are standing on a summit or trekking through a valley with no view of what's ahead.

I invite you to take a moment to pray and place your trust in God to work in your limitations. Communicate trust by inviting God to work in your life as He chooses. I need His help, and so do you. Will you join me in turning to Him right now?

"Lord, I want to talk to You about some of the limitations I'm facing. Of course, You already know what they are; but I want to admit to You that I've been hurt by my limitations, and I've questioned Your love for me because of them. I haven't understood why You, as my Friend, would allow some of these circumstances in my life. Some came as a result of things I couldn't control; some I caused by my own sins or poor decisions; and some have seemed to come simply as a result of life happening. Right now, I want to thank You, Lord, because You have taken care of me so faithfully in the past. You've healed me, touched my relationships, solved problems, and changed situations. Forgive me for losing sight of Your faithfulness. I see it now, and I thank You. I acknowledge that, just as you've done in the past, You can address my current issues, no matter how oppressive they seem—no matter how stuck I feel. I put my trust in You to work in my limitations as You choose, and I leave everything to You. Thank You for doing it. In Jesus' name, amen."

Now that you've prayed, I want to encourage you to let go of any condemnation you may be carrying as a result of the way you've handled your limitations up to this point. Think about Peter. He was a man who betrayed Jesus three times as He was on His way to be tortured and crucified, and yet God still chose Peter to be one of the most visible leaders of the exploding global movement of Jesus' followers. After Jesus rose from the dead, He met with Peter and gave him a chance to declare his love three times. In this way, Jesus restored Peter. Then, He gave Peter a three-fold assignment: "Feed my lambs, take care of my sheep, feed my sheep [Be my leader!]" (John 21:15-17, NIV). Do you see that? We may not always deal with life gracefully, but God works with us, no matter how pronounced we may feel our flaws are, and He still has plans for us.

Of course, after Peter worked faithfully to fulfill the plans God had for him, he wound up in Herod's prison with a trial date and possible execution in store. Though he had seen God work in miraculous ways before—even through his, Peter's, own hands—I'm sure one of the many emotions Peter had to battle in prison was frustration. We don't often defeat frustration in one blow; victory over frustration is a process for which we need stamina. For, after we've prayed, cultivated a heart of gratitude to God, and decided to put our trust in Him, we still wake up in the prison. After a while, being in the prison begins to wear us out. We may trust God as our Friend, but we can't deny the prison. Whatever we do to draw near to God, there is still the nagging realities of our chains and our own weariness. We end up saying what I said to God in frustration that one New Year's Eve: "Lord, I'm tired of this. I'm ready to SEE something!"

Mapping Your Next Level Leadership Journey

MILE MARKER: WHERE AM I ON THE JOURNEY?

The leader's life is full of twists and turns. If your life is anything like mine, the plans seldom go quite as planned! Like Peter in Acts 12, we end up locked into a limiting situation that we just didn't see coming.

What are you facing that limits your leadership journey?

_____

_____

_____

_____

_____

Are you in a place that's not where you had planned to go?

_____

_____

_____

_____

_____

Is it taking longer to extend your influence, complete your training, or discover your destiny than you ever imagined?

_____

_____

_____

_____

_____

Write out some of the responses to the questions above in your journal.

CHARTING YOUR COURSE: FOCUSING ON THE PATH AHEAD

The second heart attitude is a heart of gratitude. Take a moment and give thanks for every delay, every turn, and every change that has taken place. As a leader, it's critical to be able to be grateful for the things that DID NOT go according to plan. Take this moment to think of God's grace through every issue. God's mercy when you have felt like you've failed, and His love when you've felt undeserving, have been constant.

Look ahead to your journey with great anticipation, knowing that, no matter the path ahead, the journey will build your friendship with God, and you will succeed in His purposes. His unquestionable presence with you this far is your guarantee. Every time the journey has taken an unplanned—and often unwanted—turn, God has been equipping you to lead more effectively.

LEADER'S PRAYER: ASKING FOR GUIDANCE

"Lord, thank You for remaining present during my times of change, distraction, and disappointment. Thank You for causing everything in my life to work together for my good. I recommit my leadership journey to You, and I renew my trust in You and Your ways for me. Teach me to follow You when I don't fully see what You may be doing in the moment. In Jesus' name, amen."

LEADER'S WORD: RECEIVING GUIDANCE FROM HIS WORD

"*You can make many plans, but the LORD's purpose will prevail.*" —*Proverbs 19:21 (NLT)*

CHAPTER 4

STAMINA IN LIMITATIONS

I graduated from high school at 17, one in a class of about 100 in my East Tennessee town. When I walked across the stage at commencement, I was handed my diploma by a gentleman who headed one of the nation's premier nuclear engineering departments at a nearby university. He said to me, "Courtney, if they don't want you at MIT, then you come on over to us." It was a quasi-prophetic remark, as I would discover.

A few weeks later, I boarded a flight for Boston. I had been invited to participate in a summer transition program at the Massachusetts Institute of Technology before the fall semester began, and I was grateful—for, when I arrived, I found myself intimidated to the core. There I was, a kid (and I mean *a kid*—I was still six months away from turning 18!) who had excelled in every math and science class offered at my small-town high school, and now I was surrounded by students who were graduates of the Bronx High School of Science and every other major science and technology high school in America. I was intimidated academically. I was intimidated socially. And, at least initially, I felt isolated spiritually.

Slowly, I began to realize that I eventually might be as capable as some of the other students; but for me, with my lack of preparation, survival was going to be a matter of endurance. I felt the same way when I played football in ninth grade. I was small—4' 11" and 96 lbs.—while the other players weighed in at 150-200 lbs. The only way I could last and hope to remain on the team was by refusing to give up. Four years later at MIT, I was faced with the same scenario, only with crazy stakes added. Every day, I had to make the decision that I wasn't going to give up—and sometimes, I had to make it four, five, six times a day.

At first, fighting just to tread water seemed to work. I survived the pass-fail regimen of freshman year. I made some friends and, early on, found a church. Mind you, I didn't have a decent winter coat. I couldn't afford good gloves. Sometimes, I had to stand on the street and ask God to prompt someone to stop and take me to church. But I was carving out a place for myself—if just barely.

By sophomore year, even that wasn't enough. Once I started being graded in earnest, things quickly went downhill. At the end of the first semester, I found myself on academic probation. The school gave me an ultimatum: get my grades up or leave. Right about then, I remembered the words of the man who had given me my high school diploma: *If MIT doesn't want you, then come on over to us.*

Please understand: the pressure at MIT was out of this world. People were jumping out of windows over grades. Thankfully, the thought of suicide due to unacceptable grades didn't compute for me, probably in part because I didn't come from a family of high-achieving college graduates. My parents never even attended college, although my mother went to nursing school later in life. While many of my peers faced tremendous outside pressure to succeed, I had the luxury of facing failure in a way that was relatively matter-of-fact. I could just go home to Tennessee and get a degree from a different school.

I weighed the option multiple times daily. Why shouldn't I leave? What was wrong with choosing another good option? Just because a person isn't suicidal doesn't mean he isn't feeling the heat. I was as frustrated and fed up with my limitations as I could be. I'd had enough of the academic "vise," enough standing out in the cold waiting on rides, enough staying up late who-knows-how-many nights just to make grades that were insufficient to keep me there. I was worn out with my limitations. Why not just take the easier way out?

FOUR SQUADS

Why, at certain times in life, does it seem like drama, struggle, and crisis mass-produce? As soon as we've started trying to resolve drama in one area of our lives, people start fighting like cats and dogs in another area. Issues, conflicts, failures, betrayals, bad news—a whole regiment of limitations comes marching toward us all at once. Our blood pressure numbers go sky-high. Our nerves feel strung as tight as a tennis racket. Frustration becomes as normal a presence in our lives as the air we breathe. We wonder if God has stepped out on us.

You know what it's like. There's a reason for the cliché, "When it rains, it pours."

I'm sure Peter could relate. Not only had the church witnessed the loss of one of its faithful and effective leaders, Stephen, in a bloody, public stoning; not only did followers of Jesus get dragged from their homes, tortured, and killed under Peter's watch; not only did the believers leave Jerusalem in droves, causing the church temporarily to lose its geographical center; not only did Herod arrest and kill Peter's friend and fellow leader, James; but now, Peter himself had been arrested, taken to prison, and possibly marked for death.

Even that wasn't all. Once Peter actually got to the prison, he faced a serious contingent of Herod's men. Security went way beyond those two guards chained to Peter while he slept. You would think two would've been enough—it's not like Peter could go anywhere. But the Bible says Herod assigned four squads of soldiers to Peter. Those two men chained on either side of him were part of a much bigger security detail set up to cover Peter, probably in shifts around the clock.

So what is "four squads of soldiers"? It is four groups of four, or 16 men, usually working in rotating shifts of four men each—and those in addition to all the regular prison guards and wardens. I don't know about you, but I need some help understanding this. What kind of man needs all those guards when he's already in prison? This is not a guerrilla fighter or a highly-positioned political leader. This is not the leader of a crime ring. This is Peter, an apostle, ex-fisherman, and preacher—the leader of what they saw as a persecuted, scattered religious sect that would soon pass away.

If Peter and his followers weren't a threat, then tell me why Herod put that kind of security detail on him. I bet Peter was wondering the same thing: *Why all the fuss; why all the soldiers? I'm not even armed. As a matter of fact, I'm not even that good with a sword. Ask my friends. I wanted to cut a man's jugular vein in Gethsemane when he was threatening Jesus, and I cut his ear off instead. Missed his whole neck and got his ear. Yeah, I'm good with a fishing net, but I'm pretty sorry with a weapon. So what's the deal with all of this?*

The other prisoners had to have been just as perplexed. Let's say I'm a prisoner in the next cell: I'm watching these men march by with Peter, and I'm wondering, *Why does a preacher need all these guards? What has he done? Not one of us has that kind of security. What do they think he's going to do? What kind of backup does this man have? What's up with this guy?*

Now, let's bridge this scene to your life and limitations. You may be in the same position as Peter. Maybe it seems as if things have been going bad for years: raining, pouring—even monsooning, as far as you're concerned. Now, you're constrained, chained up in your personal prison; on top of it all, you're surrounded by guards. Guards of discouragement. Guards of anxiety. Guards of I-don't-have-what-it-takes. Your head is spinning just from looking at the rows of guards. You wonder if you're about to lose your mind.

But I wonder what onlookers are thinking when they see you sitting in your cell. There you are in your limiting, frustrating situation, surrounded by squads of potentially debilitating circumstances, asking yourself, *Why all the trouble? Why all the struggle? Why all the stuff blocking me? Why all the soldiers of discouragement attached to me?* Meanwhile, as with the hypothetical prisoner in the cell next to Peter's, it may be that the people watching your life have greater insight than you do. While you're sitting there wondering if the unrelenting pressure and the ongoing streak of difficult circumstances are signs that your life is cursed, I'm here to tell you that some of those same difficulties may be signs that your life is *blessed*.

SEEING THINGS DIFFERENTLY

Half the battle against frustration is seeing things differently—in fact, it's probably more than half the battle. The way we see things can make or break our ability to endure, and it can directly influence our destiny. Before the time came for Israel to cross the Jordan and enter the Promised Land, Moses sent a group of spies into the territory on a 40-day reconnaissance mission. These spies sized up the land and came back with a report. First, they told of the land's abundance, displaying a sampling of fruit they had to carry on a pole: "[The land] certainly does flow with milk and honey," the men said, "and this is its fruit" (Numbers 13:27, NASB).

But then, the spies switched up. You would think they would've given a little more detail about the terrain, the soil, the water supply—something. After years of God talking to them about the Promised Land—about the splendid cities and olive groves and houses—you would think the spies would've had a little more to say. How about showing some respect for God by sharing a few of the details? No. A general, "Yes, the land's got milk and honey," was all the people got before the spies changed gears. You can see the switch coming by looking at the very next word in the passage: "Nevertheless." The spies were saying, "The land's great and all, just like God said, but ...." But *what*?

Here's what they went on to explain: "Nevertheless, the people who live in the land are strong, and the cities are fortified and very large; and moreover, we saw the descendants of Anak there ... and all the people whom we saw ... are men of great size" (Numbers 13:28, 32, NASB). Look at that detail! At least we know the spies were capable of observation. But what were they saying? They were saying the land was full of giants—and, in the minds of the spies, those giants were so great in size that they obscured everything else. All the spies could see were the obstacles.

Ultimately, the spies chose to see their prospects one way—as impossible. "We became like grasshoppers in our own sight," they told the people (Numbers 13:33, NASB). That was the faith killer—the way they saw themselves. Next thing you know, all the people began to see themselves and their chances the same way. The word on taking the Promised Land was, "Fold. Give up. It's not worth it." Nobody but two dissenting spies, Joshua and Caleb, wanted to go in. The result? God had to let that entire generation die out—which required another 40 years in the wilderness—so He could get some people who would see things differently.

The way I saw things at MIT could have easily changed the course of my life. God is sovereign in our lives—He is in control at all times—but He also respects our free will. Our decisions may not ultimately stop God from fulfilling His plans, but our choices can prevent us from enjoying those plans as He originally laid them out. At MIT, everything was set up to make me see myself the way those spies saw themselves in the land. I was failing to meet academic standards. I didn't have two dimes to rub together. My suits were so thin I could feel my own breath through the sleeves, let alone that bone-rattling Boston wind. It was all set up to make me see myself as a poor country kid who didn't belong, who couldn't make the cut, who would never take the land. If I had embraced that view, my life might have followed a different route. But somehow, in my fog of frustration, when nothing seemed to be going my way, I managed to hang on in faith, believing God had a purpose for me at MIT and remembering who I was: God's friend. Seeing things rightly—seeing myself rightly—is what kept me at least partially sane and persevering in my limitations.

Now, let's return to Peter's ordeal. We're never told how Peter was seeing things when all those guards were marshaling him into his cell. We have no idea whether Peter was battling despair or believing God for a miracle. What we can do is gauge the way Herod might have seen things. Judging from the way he set things up in the prison, it's safe to say Herod might have seen more potential in Peter than Peter did in himself. That's why he assigned all the guards. Herod knew the man he had arrested. This wasn't Peter, the ex-fisherman, the inconsequential preacher. This was Peter: God's chosen leader, miracle worker, mobilizer of thousands, preacher whose speech could cut people to the heart. Herod got it. He knew exactly whom he was dealing with. Herod was seeing things rightly.

One thing to remember is that, even when you can't seem to see things with eyes of faith, you have an enemy who can. I'm not talking about that coworker who keeps talking about you behind your back. I'm not referring to some of your crazy relatives, either! I don't mean a person. I mean the devil. The devil understands more about your potential—has more faith in your potential—than you do. He knows the truth. He knows that God isn't waiting around to empower you someday way off in the future. God has *already* empowered you. You are who God says you are right now. Not after you get married. Not after you buy your own home. Not after you get the next job. Not when you have more money. You are who God says you are before any of that. As God's friend, you're at the Next Level right where you are—and the devil knows it.

In fact, the enemy is so frightened by who you are that he's working overtime. He has placed whole attachments and brigades and squads of frustrating, limiting—even devastating—circumstances around you just so he can prevent you from seeing who you really are: God's empowered friend. He knows that, if you see it, your potential is as good as realized. He's saying, "I'm in trouble if she ever sees her potential. I'm dead if he ever knows who he is."

But I've got good news for you and bad news for the devil: it's too late! Right now, we're beginning to see things differently. Right now, we're awakening to who we really are—the friends of God, invested with everything we need to fulfill His plans for our lives. We're no longer seeing ourselves as victims. Rather than staying discouraged about the squads of soldiers, we're actually becoming happy about them. Every time I see another hindrance, I can exercise that second Next Level heart attitude—a heart of gratitude to God—and say, "Lord, thank You for helping me see things correctly. That hindrance can be another confirmation that I'm important to You, another confirmation that You're doing something powerful with my life," and,

"Thank You, Lord—even though the enemy is bringing things against me, You're going to use those trials to bring out my potential."

I need to be as smart about me as the devil is about me. I need to get in the faces of all my guards and say, "The only reason you're in my life is because God is taking me on an incredible journey in friendship, and the fact that you're here just confirms it!"

KEYS TO TRANSFORMING OUR FRUSTRATION

If seeing things differently is half the battle against frustration, then the other half is learning to daily face down our frustration. I can't tell you how many times at MIT I cried out to God, "Do I ever get to graduate?" I didn't mean graduate from MIT. I meant graduate from CDS—Character Development School. Yes, I believed I was God's friend. I believed God had plans for me, both in and beyond the struggle. I believed God was on my side. That didn't mean I wanted to stay in the prison. "Get me out of here, Lord!" was my take on things; but the wearisome, depressing dynamics of much of my daily life could wear down my morale in about 20 seconds.

The Bible says we should rejoice in limitations because the testing of our faith produces endurance (James 1:2-3). Well, at least we know our limitations are producing the very thing we need to survive them—stamina! With that in mind, there are some things we can do to mitigate the frustration that gets in our way. Let's look at some keys that will help us transform our frustrations, take hold of peace, and build stamina for the rest of our "jail term."

Worship

By worship, I do not mean what we do in a church service. Singing, giving offerings, participating in the liturgy, lifting our hands—these are all expressions of worship. However, 'm talking about worship as a lifestyle: the way we live in God and respond to what life brings.

Consider Peter sleeping between those two guards. The complete verse reads, "On the very night when Herod was about to bring him forward, Peter was sleeping between two soldiers, bound with two chains, and guards in front of the door were watching over the prison" (Acts 12:6, NASB).

Whatever emotions he had to battle, Peter sleeping in prison the night before his trial is a picture of worship. Why? Because it is a picture of trust, surrender, and rest—the posture of the worshipper's heart. When we rest in God, we are saying with our hearts that He is God and we are not; He is all-powerful, all-knowing, and never limited. We trust Him to take care of us; we believe He is in control. Our rest in difficult moments makes a statement that God is greater than our limitations and deserving of our worship.

Rest is also evidence of our second Next Level heart attitude, a heart of gratitude to God. As we thank God—not just for what He has done, but also for who He is—our anxiety subsides, and we can more readily rest in Him. In this way, gratitude builds intimacy with God. Why don't you try it? You can say, "God, I thank You for who You are to me—the Lover of my soul, my Bread when I'm hungry, my Water when I'm thirsty. You're my Lawyer in the courtroom, my Doctor in the sickroom, my help in times of trouble, my Friend when I'm lonely and friendless. You lift my heart when I'm discouraged. You're my

Provider, my Wonderful Counselor, my Prince of Peace, my All in All. I just want to thank You, God. You're more extraordinary than I could ever describe."

Worship becomes easier as I remember that a mighty, all-loving, all-knowing God is taking care of me. Gratitude to Him, love, rest, trust—these all work together in the worshipper's heart, building stamina in limitations and, more than just stamina, real peace. Peter learned it from Jesus, who slept in that boat with the disciples even as it was sinking in the storm. Now, more than a decade later, Peter took the opportunity to rest, trust, worship, and sleep in his own storm-tossed boat—his heavily-guarded prison cell.

When we come to a place where we trust God enough that we can sleep in the face of what appears to be a death sentence, then we become dangerous to the enemy. You are a threat when you can say, "God, You know what? If You give me the money, I'm going to rejoice; and if You don't give me the money, I'm still going to rejoice. While I'm in my apartment—while I'm still living in the projects—while I'm hurting in this relationship—I'm still going to give You praise." Anybody can praise God in the mansion, when you get the job, when you get the promotion, when you get the ring, when you're experiencing the external blessings for which you long; however, it takes a real worshipper to stand in the midst of limitations, when God is digging into his or her life and making internal changes, and say, "God, I feel limited right now. I don't see what I long for coming to pass. It looks like it's not happening. But I will bless you at all times, and your 'praise shall continually be in my mouth' " (Psalm 34:1, NASB). When you come to that place—where you no longer fear what the enemy can do to you and you can fall asleep with all of those guards standing over you—you become a dangerous man or woman.

What if I want to worship God, trusting and resting the way Peter did, but I can't seem to do it? What if I'm just too wound up? Limitations, storms, pressures—these can take a toll on our minds and bodies. We may want to go to sleep between our guards, but we find ourselves suffering the physical and emotional effects of stress, anxiety, anger, and frustration—effects we can't control. We can't seem to make ourselves rest in God, and we feel guilty, as if we've failed in our faith. *I must not really love God*, we think. *Why can't I worship Him in trouble like others seem able to do?*

God sees you and understands where you are. The Bible says He is "intimately acquainted" with all your ways (Psalm 139:3). He understands your mind, your body, and the way your limitations are wearing on you. Resting in God, worshipping Him, taking hold of peace in difficult times—this is not an easy business. It is hard to settle down in the midst of frustration, drama, or chaos and enjoy the journey of friendship with God. Sometimes, it is a moment-by-moment endeavor. But the struggle doesn't mean you are losing; it doesn't mean you are weak or deficient. The struggle means you've embraced your friendship with God and put your faith in His ability to carry you out of your limitations if He so chooses. You're struggling precisely because you are fighting the impulse to see things like those spies did. Don't lose heart! God is on your side. He is working in that storm, and He will help you into peace.

In the meantime, don't condemn yourself if you can't seem to rest in God as you wish. Sometimes, worshipping is simply a matter of expressing one's desire to do so: "God, I know I belong to You. I want my life to be an expression of worship to You. I want to trust You. I want to rest. Help me." This is your part—to decide to worship, and then to constantly renew your decision. God must take care of the rest—literally.

"Forget" the Past

When we find ourselves in a limited place, we can get stuck dwelling on the past. Peter had plenty of time to sit there thinking. When we feel trapped, static, or caught in a waiting posture, all kinds of thoughts can seep into our minds. We may start longing to go back to some relationship or season of life that God ended. We may spend hours meditating on the circumstances that landed us in our limitations. Before we know it, our hearts are filled with hurt, frustration, anger, sorrow, blame, condemnation, fear, or all of the above.

Paul wrote, "One thing I do: forgetting what lies behind and reaching forward to what lies ahead, I press on toward the goal for the prize of the upward call of God in Christ Jesus" (Philippians 3:13-14, NASB). Forget what lies behind. Paul had to "forget" so he could "press on." As long as you are holding on to what's behind you, you are hindered in reaching forward. If you go after the past, you will end up staying in the past.

As one of the first African American kids to integrate my little elementary school in Tennessee in the 1960s, I must've been called racial epithets many times. Now, I have to work to remember even one instance. Truly, I have forgotten—and I thank God, because if I had stayed in that emotional place, meditating on those moments and scenes, I would've forgotten who God says I am. Certain memories can paralyze us if we don't choose to release them. Jesus cautioned, "Remember Lot's wife" (Luke 17:32). She became a pillar of salt when she turned to look back.

If Paul could decide to forget the past, then we must have the right to decide, as well. Of course, some things cannot be forgotten as in wiped from our memory. By "forgetting," we really mean stripping the past of its power to hold us. We can make up our minds to do that: *I'm going to quit meditating on the past, quit turning my past mistakes over in my head, quit sifting through old hurts and the memories that haunt me.* Once we make that decision, we ask God to help us. Just as with our decision to rest in God, we may need to renew this decision regularly, constantly calling on God for help. As we do this, He works with us, freeing us to experience peace.

Part of letting go of the past is forgiving. Holding unforgiveness in our hearts keeps us chained to the past and in pent up frustration. When we don't forgive others, we keep dragging them and the hurts around like proverbial albatrosses around our necks. We can't move ahead, our frustration only continues to build, and we suffer.

Right now, you can make a decision to forgive those who hurt you—even if the one you need to forgive is yourself. You may continue to deal with anger and other emotions, but make the decision to forgive. If you are struggling to do that, spend some time meditating on God's gift of forgiveness. Think about what that gift cost—what Jesus suffered so we could have it. Since God has forgiven us at the cost of His own Son, we too must be willing to forgive. Ask God to help you make the decision. As with other spiritual decisions, you may have to keep renewing this one; however, the more determined you are to hold on to God, the less strength you are using to hold on to the hurt.

What if I can't "forget" the past? What if I want to let go, but the memories keep coming back? This is real. Some hurts cut deeply, and the healing process takes time. Be patient with yourself. Lean on God. You may need to seek help from others in the process, such as family members, friends, or counselors. Meanwhile, as you wait on God to do His part in healing you, allow whatever is "haunting" you to strengthen your dependence on Him. Let the pain drive you to God. Your ability to trust Him will grow, and your friendship with Him will deepen.

Make Plans

Sometimes, we can ease our frustration simply by making plans. Often, we walk around thinking about the dreams in our hearts and the plans we long to see come to pass, but we fail to be proactive about pursuing them. Maybe we're afraid of failure. Maybe we feel constrained by our present limitations or by what we see as our own deficiencies. Maybe we don't believe that God wants to fulfill our dreams. Maybe we fear making a wrong move and displeasing God. We certainly want to proceed carefully and prayerfully, but continued inaction can add to our frustration. If we remain passive, we run the risk of giving up on our dreams altogether.

Bring your dreams and goals to God and ask Him to direct you. Ask Him to help you understand which of your goals line up with His. Then, consider how you can plan to take steps in the direction of some of them. Have you been thinking seriously about getting out of debt? What is your strategy to begin tackling the process? Do you want to be married? How can you become proactive about nurturing the friendships God has already given you? Do you want to go back to school? Have you begun researching your options? Limitations can become so debilitating that we stop acting, moving, and pursuing our goals. But prayerfully making plans and taking steps—even small steps—relieves frustration and renews our hope.

RESISTING THE TEMPTATION TO BAIL

After all the heartache and strain of my MIT experience, I ended up staying on and graduating in four years. The key to my success turned out to be a totally unforeseen academic alternative. At some point when I was on academic probation, I must've come across a sign or a note that alerted me to a new major being offered. I could still take my core engineering courses but also pursue coursework in humanities. With my personality, strengths, and interests, this new major was a much better fit for me. Almost immediately, my grades made a quantum leap (no pun intended) and, as it turned out, the saving alternative proved to be a significant part of God's plan. The new major equipped me much more suitably for the field in engineering that I later entered, and I would've missed a vital part of my preparation had I bailed out early.

In the tightest places of your life, God can open doors to rich, legacy-building opportunities. As much as you want out, there is a great chance that what's happening with you right now is essential preparation for what lies ahead on your path of life. Don't cut the process short.

Had I left MIT, I might have missed a lot more than critical vocational preparation; right there, in that limited place, I met my wife, Janeen, God's greatest blessing to me! Resist the temptation to bail out early. Hold on where you are. Apply the keys to transforming frustration, so you don't lose your mind—worship God, "forget" the past, make plans—and keep seeing yourself correctly, as God's empowered friend. There is a great deal ahead for you on the journey.

Mapping Your Next Level Leadership Journey

MILE MARKER: WHERE AM I ON THE JOURNEY?

Think about some of the "guards" in your "prison cell of limitation." They may seem to loom larger than life and create a sense of inadequacy for you, especially in your leadership arena. The truth is that God is giving you stamina in the midst of the journey so you can live through where you are. Things may be going very well, but you still long for a life with no limits.

How can you increase strength here at this critical place in your journey?

_____

_____

_____

_____

_____

CHARTING YOUR COURSE: FOCUSING ON THE PATH AHEAD

As you continue, God will strengthen you for the journey. His power is perfected in our weakness. He gives strength to those who need it most, if we'll just ask Him. As you view the path ahead, view it in faith. You are called to lead others, and it will require you to operate in the strength of the Lord, even when you may be weak. From the place of limitations, see yourself becoming strong as you worship, forget the past, and make plans for the future!

LEADER'S PRAYER: ASKING FOR GUIDANCE

"Lord, I need Your strength to prosper in times of limitation. I want to lead out of the overflow of my friendship with You. Teach me, in this season of my life, to draw close and inhale the extra oxygen of Your presence that adds stamina to my daily journey. Thank You for neither leaving me nor distancing Yourself from a sinner like me. In Jesus' name, amen."

LEADER'S WORD: RECEIVING GUIDANCE FROM HIS WORD

"The Lord will guide you continually, giving you water when you are dry and restoring your strength. You will be like a well-watered garden, like an ever-flowing spring." —Isaiah 58:11 (NLT)

CHAPTER 5

YOUR DESIGNER PRISON

Norfolk, Virginia. The mid-1990s. I was sitting in the city jail, trying to imagine how I was going to feel spending time in here. This was a cell, not the waiting area. The room was cold, colorless. I was locked in with a few other men and had begun to feel claustrophobic. But I was the one who had made the decision to be here. I had made choices and, whether I liked it or not, I would have to accept the consequences. Thankfully, I was only in for a couple of hours to preach to some men who had lost their way. Oh, you thought …. No. I hadn't. But I was in jail.

My wife and I had come to Norfolk in 1990 to establish Calvary Revival Church, the church we still lead today. After MIT and a few more years in Boston, Janeen and I moved first to Tennessee, where I continued to work as an engineer. We had three children during the

Boston-Tennessee years. Shortly after birth, one of our sons nearly died, and I lost my mother to cancer when she was just 44. A few years later, I turned down a promotion to senior management with my company and, at 30, relocated my family to the Hampton Roads area of Virginia. I had no job waiting for me, a fourth child on the way, and very few contacts—but I also had a sense that God was calling my family and me to plant a church in Norfolk.

What started as a weekly meeting in a hotel conference room with some 21 folks quickly mushroomed, and we changed locations several times. In 1991, we began meeting in a rented retail space some might refer to as a "storefront." During that period—about seven years—we continued to focus our efforts on reaching out to the community. I named our prison ministry the "Jonah Ministry" because, as I went on to explain to the group of men who gathered for our service at the Norfolk City Jail, even as the fish that swallowed Jonah became his life preserver, so the jail or prison could become theirs. Without the fish, Jonah would have drowned. Jail was a tight place, a lonely place—but it was better than the grave.

Moreover, I told the men, God had plans for them. God had determined that they wouldn't die in an armed robbery, perish in a drug raid, or be gunned down by friend or foe. Instead, God was rerouting and rebuilding them through the penal system. He was making the jail experience a "designer prison"—one that would work for their good. The same is true for you. You may have landed in limitation for any number of reasons; but right there, in your cell, God is preserving you, fixing you, building you, and using your limitations to prepare you for the coming phases of your journey.

I've seen God do it for me. At about that same time, in the mid-90s, I was experiencing tight, limited places in my own life. My young family had grown from three kids to five in just a few years, and our house was now a pretty tight place. Our church, too, seemed to be bursting at the seams as we tried to accommodate the lines of people wrapped around our rented building for each of three Sunday services, only to have to turn many folk away. We were battling for permission to build a larger church facility on land we had purchased, but things were not going our way. Intense feelings of isolation and helplessness became the daily fare as we seemed to make little progress. Still, I kept my eyes on God, trusting that we were "locked up" in limitations He was tailoring for our benefit.

Looking back at that period of ministry now, it seems clear that God had us right where He wanted us. Certain vital aspects of my character were forged under that pressure. Only God knew that a time was coming when I would need to trust Him for greater resources, influence, and favor. Only God knew that we would eventually serve many more people locally, provide leadership and assistance to ministries worldwide, broadcast a global television outreach, and impact various civic entities. Sitting in my designer prison, I had no idea what was coming—but God, the Designer, knew. He knew exactly how to make my limitations work for His purposes and my good.

For instance, God used a prison in which I was ridiculed, taken lightly, and rejected by some to build my character so that I wouldn't tend to become lifted up in pride as God worked expansively through the ministry later. God made my prison work for me by using it to teach me a deeper level of dependence on Him. In my designer prison, I experienced a depth of brokenness I would never forget, but my faith expanded greatly as I watched God work in our ministry and bring us out of our limitations step-by-step. In the end, we did not build a church on our land—we built a school and later purchased a warehouse that we would convert into the church campus. But it was within the confines of an inadequate rented space that God taught me His resources and influence are unlimited.

YOU BELONG TO GOD

Is it often difficult to believe your prison could have a good purpose? Do you look at the squads of guards around you and become convinced the devil is controlling what happens to you, as if he has a license to oppress and destroy you? David wrote in the Psalms, "The earth is the Lord's, and all it contains, the world, and those who live in it" (Psalm 24:1, NASB). If the earth and all it contains belong to God, then the prison, too, must be under His authority. The devil doesn't rule your life—you belong to God.

David also wrote: "Where can I go from Your Spirit? Or where can I flee from Your presence?" (Psalm 139:7, NASB) There is no place the devil can drag you off to that will hide you from God. Maybe you believe yourself so broken down, damaged, and hemmed in that God can't get to you. Perhaps you feel trapped emotionally and out of God's reach. I want to encourage you: there is no place, no prison, no emotional dungeon that is hidden from the Lord. When the enemy tries to limit your life, he is still under God's authority—and so are you. If God says, "Enough," then the devil must go.

Before he attacked Job, the enemy had to get permission from God. God made the ground rules. It went something like this: "Understand me, devil. I'm not going to let you do anything that will destroy Job. Whatever you do to him, I will turn it around and make it work for his good. If I give you room to maneuver in his life, it's only because I love him. He may not see it that way. He may not understand. But if I let you through the gate, then I will make you work for the good of my son. You will not take him out. You will not destroy him. I've already equipped and prepared him for whatever you bring."

If the devil puts you in prison, he must put you there with God's knowledge. And since God already sees your prison as a designer prison, when the enemy drags you off, he just drags you further into God's purpose for your life. The Bible says, "And we know that God causes all things to work together for good to those who love God, to those who are called according to His purpose" (Romans 8:28, NASB). That means that whatever trial, affliction, sorrow, challenge, or sudden trauma comes your way, God has already arranged to work it for your good. That can be a hard pill to swallow when you're in prison and you just want out; but it's true—your limitations are working for you.

For instance, maybe at some point you performed poorly in an area of your job. The enemy thought that, through discouragement, he could shut down your productivity, but God had already planned to use your weak performance to help you become more creative and tenacious and to drive you to an even higher level of achievement than you would've reached otherwise. Maybe there was a time when someone you loved left you. The enemy thought it was over for you emotionally, but God had already planned to use what happened to strengthen and prepare you for a healthier, more fulfilling relationship in the future.

God also may allow limitations to come upon us because we don't have enough sense or foresight to stay in His will without them. God may put limitations on us to keep us from doing something wild and crazy. He may put us "on lock" to keep us from running off somewhere. Maybe that's why the job promotion didn't happen for you. Maybe that's why the change of assignment didn't come through. Maybe you missed it because God didn't want you to move to another city. You know how we are—we'll do it our own way. We'll go where we want to go. We'll fall in love with whomever we want to fall in love with. Sometimes, God puts limitations on us in order to keep us on the path of life—not because He hates us, but because He loves us.

IT'S A SETUP

Here's the problem: we think that, because we're in prison, God is limited in what He can do in our lives. But our limitations become a setup for God.

Think back to Peter for a moment. Herod may have given the orders to place four squads of soldiers in shifts around Peter, but Herod was under God's authority. God was fully aware of the security build-up. Who knows? Maybe Herod said, "Only chain one guard to Peter's side," but the Holy Spirit said, "Put two on him." Herod might've said, "Give the guards a break when night falls, because the prisoner will be asleep." But maybe the Lord said, "No, no. I want those guards chained to him because I prepare a table for My servants in the presence of their enemies, and it won't glorify Me if there aren't any enemies around when My angel shows up."

I can hear the angel saying, "May I go now, Lord? May I go get Peter out?"

And the Lord saying, "Not yet."

"But in two days, they're going to kill him, Lord."

"I said, 'Wait.'"

Then later, the angel: "Now may I go? There's only one day left."

And God: "No."

And again: "May I go now? It's only 18 hours."

And again: "No."

Finally, the angel sits down, thinking, "Well, it looks like Peter's coming up here after all."

But just before daybreak, the order comes down: "Go get him out now."

Can you see how God works? He waits for the optimal moment; at times, that may mean He waits until things look the darkest so He can set up our circumstances to do something spectacular.

Keep in mind too that, by this time, Peter was sleeping. Sometimes, God will wait on you to fall asleep because He's tired of you trying to help im. He needs you to be still. He needs you to say, "God, I know You've got this under control, so I'm going to rest now. I'm tired of worrying. I'm tired of being nervous. I'm tired of taking pills to go to sleep and pills to get up. I'm tired of walking around like I've lost my mind. I'm tired of this, Lord. I'm going to rest right here and wait on You."

That may be just what God wants from you. His thought may be, "I need you to sit still because, if you try to be My co-pilot, you may think you actually got yourself free. You just sit back and watch. I've got you covered—even if I walk in at the very last minute."

Do you know God will do just that? He'll walk in once you've given up, thrown in the towel, and said it looks impossible. He'll walk in once others have told you to forget it. He'll set up your prison, your chains, your guards, and then, just as soon as your demise looks imminent, He will walk in.

GOD DESIGNS THE PRISON JUST FOR YOU

What I love about God is that He doesn't need good materials to make good stuff; He can take intrinsically bad or limiting materials and make them good. If you examine your life, I bet you will find that God has taken limiting circumstances, relationships, habits, or dysfunctions and created something beneficial for you or for others. That's a good moment to take a "praise break" and exercise our second Next Level heart attitude—a heart of gratitude to God. When I consider our struggle years ago to build the church on our property, and then I drive by our K-12 school campus located there today, I can't help but thank God. All it takes is a little interaction with a few of the students whose lives are being built up there to remind me that God can redeem limitations and use them to produce wonderful results.

It's not just that God works around or in spite of our limitations. He actually works with our limitations, designing them to bring us maximum benefit and growth. In God's hands, our limitations can develop us to the fullest degree and prepare us for purpose in the coming phases of our journey. God has His eye on our strengths and weaknesses; He knows both the plans that He has for us and the character we need to fulfill those plans. "Before I formed you in the womb I knew you," God told Jeremiah (Jeremiah 1:5, NASB). If some weakness or undeveloped area is in the way of what God wants to do in our lives, He may design our limitations to address and strengthen that area.

Which of your weaknesses are becoming clearer to you under the pressure of limitations? In what areas of your character can you feel yourself changing and growing? Ask God to give you wisdom about the weak areas He wants to address in your life, so you can cooperate with His loving work. The prison isn't a sign that God has rejected you. God loves you and chose you to be His friend. He is designing and working uniquely in your prison so it becomes the place of your growth. This is a way God redeems your limitations—His work in your prison is a sign of His love.

God works uniquely too in the lives of your friends and loved ones. Even as you have your designer prison, so your friends and family have theirs. Resist the temptation to compare your tough times with what may look like the relative ease of others. You may want to say, "She isn't going through what I'm going through. He doesn't know what I know. I've got a Ph.D. in prison living. They don't get it." However, as much as you want to toe that line, resist. God's plans for others are not the same as His plans for you. God molds and designs your prison so it will prepare you for your ongoing journey, and He works in the lives and limitations of others to best prepare them for theirs.

THE PRISON BECOMES A PLACE FOR FRIENDSHIP

All of us understand, on some level, what it feels like to be isolated. Peter's prison was probably built into the outer wall of the city—that is, he was removed from people and activity. I can imagine him there, longing for his city; longing to be part of its life; longing for the people who loved him; longing to be with them, to draw strength from them, and to do what he did best: lead them. Sometimes, the cruelest part of being in prison is enduring the loneliness—the feeling that we are by ourselves with no one to lean on. Yet while we are alone, God affords us the opportunity to rest, collect our thoughts, and learn how to live more intimately with Him. Before anything else, our prison can be a place where we grow closer to God in friendship.

David wrote in the Psalms, "For my father and my mother have forsaken me, but the Lord will take me up" (Psalm 27:10, NASB). David's parents did not forsake him as in reject him. David was telling us that, even if his father and mother had deserted him, the Lord would have taken care of him. As with David, when I am sitting in prison—isolated, lonely, forsaken—God will take me to Himself. God will be my comfort and safety. He will love me as only He can.

We fight against rejection because it hurts; we don't want to talk about it. But many times, the moment we are rejected—the moment we feel the most isolated—is the moment God is building something into us that we never would've gotten when surrounded by others. When we are alone with God outside the city, feeling desolate, useless, and without any real significance or purpose, He can step in and be everything to us. As one of His Hebrew names—El Shaddai—means, in our limitations, God can show Himself to be our All-Sufficient One.

Sometimes it is in losing things that we learn how to love God most deeply. Activities, relationships, and situations in our lives can hinder our love for God. Often, we don't see the hindrance until we experience loss. Stripped of what we thought gave us our identity, we wonder, "Am I a lost cause? Is it over for me?" We don't realize that when "mother and father" forsake us, when the people we thought were keeping us leave us, when the stuff we were leaning on can't hold us anymore, when what we thought gave us purpose and identity goes out of our lives—then God Himself will take us up. God will use our unique limitations, our designer prison, to open up springs of intimacy with Him. Loss may hurt, but if I must lose things in order to grow in my love relationship with God, then I embrace that process.

I must get to the point where that first Next Level heart attitude, my heart for friendship with God, is what flows out of me under pressure, causing me to say, "God, when it's all said and done, I trust You. If You say You love me, then right here in this prison, You love me. My mother and father, my friends, and my hopes are gone; however, if You say You love me, then I'm going to wait right here until my change comes. Even sitting in this cell with my dreams destroyed and my heart broken, I'm still loving and worshipping You, because the greatest promise I've ever received is the promise that You will walk with me and talk with me and call me Your own. As long as you do that, I have everything I need."

EMBRACING CONTENTMENT

The apostle Paul explained in one of his letters that, after asking God three times to remove a limitation, a "thorn in the flesh," from his life, he got this response: "My grace is sufficient for you, for power is perfected in weakness" (2 Corinthians 12:9, NASB).

The grace God promised to Paul was more than just an antidote for the pain of the thorn in his flesh. This grace was "sufficient," which in the Greek speaks of abundance—more than enough, not "just enough," which is the way we sometimes read the word "sufficient." God's grace to Paul was all-sufficient, just as God's name, El Shaddai, the All-Sufficient One, describes God's nature to be. Grace is more than a temporal fix or strength to persevere in one issue; it is an eternal answer to a lot of different issues. When we ask for help with one limitation, whether He lifts it or not, God does a whole lot more.

This means that our prison can be more than just a setup for God to do something spectacular in one area of our lives; it also becomes a setup for God to sweep through our lives in multiple areas and make adjustments. That's good news! Now I know why Paul got excited. "Most gladly, therefore," he wrote, "I will rather boast about my weaknesses, so that the power of Christ may dwell in me" (2 Corinthians 12:9, NASB). This wasn't a grin-and-bear-it response from Paul concerning his "thorn." He was saying, "Wow, if this all-sufficient grace is what you get when you're weak and limited, then let me be weak and limited!"

Prison can actually be a liberating phase in our journey. Once we settle down from the storms of frustration and settle into the lessons of the prison—letting God grow us, letting Him love us, letting Him apply His grace to our lives—we really can become expectant about God's grace, as Paul did, and come to a place of contentment in the process.

Paul wrote, "Now godliness with contentment is great gain" (1 Timothy 6:6, NKJV). Contentment doesn't mean being satisfied with the status quo or ignoring one's desire for change. Contentment can be preparation for change. Godliness plus contentment gains momentum and moves us into position for the next phase of the journey. I don't know about you, but I want to be in position! Let's consider some ways we can embrace contentment.

Come Out of Denial

One thing I've learned to do in limiting circumstances is to stare them in the face and refuse to hide from worst-case scenarios. Sometimes, we don't want to look at how bad things actually are or might become—because, in doing so, we become paralyzed by fear. We'd rather live in denial. But the Bible says, "For God has not given us a spirit of fear, but of power and of love and of a sound mind" (2 Timothy 1:7, NKJV). The enemy is the one keeping us terrified of the what-ifs. He keeps us in denial by holding us hostage to our fears.

Our part, then, is to refuse to be bound by the what-ifs: "What if I lose my house? What if they repossess my car?" If the enemy is trying to hold me hostage to these possibilities, then I'm just going to take him there and turn the questions back on him. "Okay, so what if they repossess my car? If that's the worst thing that can happen, then God will eventually help me get another one and, in the meantime, He'll make sure I have transportation," and, "God is my provider. He is taking care of me. If I lose my house, then He'll just find me some-where else to go."

When we come out of denial, acknowledge worst-case scenarios, and confront our fears, we call the devil's bluff. He can no longer hold us hostage if we are no longer afraid. In this sense, while sitting in prison, we're actually free. Chained up in limitations and restricting circumstances, we're released in our hearts and minds, and this kind of freedom is part of contentment. We look at where we are, and we acknowledge, "Yes, this is where I am, but I'm still alive. I'm not dead. Could it get worse? Probably. But at this point, it is what it is. I see it. I'm not trying to dress it up or shut my eyes to it. And right in the midst of it, I trust God. He loves me. He's my Friend. He's working it out for my good. And I am not afraid."

Make a Decision

Contentment, like many things in our walk with God, is a decision. I decide to be content, and I ask God to help me live out that decision. Jesus said, "Which of you by worrying can add one cubit to his stature?" (Matthew 6:27, NKJV). While the verse here actually refers to our inability by worrying to add days or length to our lifespan—not inches to our height—at just under 5' 6", I still like the idea of applying the principle to my literal stature. I realize that, if I chose, I could let worrying about my height rob me of joy and self-worth. But since I can't get any taller, why worry about it? At some point, I must make a decision to be content with 5' 5-3/4". And I have. I even relish using myself as an object lesson when I'm teaching, often remarking to audiences, "In your situation, have you ever felt small? Well, at just over 5' 5", I wake up feeling that way every day!"

Limitations can make us feel small, insignificant, and stripped of our dignity. But once we understand that we are significant to God, that we were created for Him, and that even our limitations are God's servants, making us better, drawing us closer to Him—once it clicks that our significance is not tied to our limiting circumstances but tied up in God—then, with understanding, faith, and hope, we can decide to be content. We can trust God to get the most mileage out of the limitations that seem permanent, or to free us—if that is His plan—from those that are not.

Welcome Delayed Gratification

Delay does not mean God's answer is "no." Just because God withholds something from us for a time doesn't mean He will withhold it forever. Learning to wait is one of the most important skills we can develop in prison. Just as I can choose contentment, I can choose to wait expectantly for the great things God has in store for me on the journey. In the case of our ministry, in deciding to build a school on our property, we elected to wait for God to provide the church building at a future time. Note that we waited actively. We welcomed God's timing for the church, but we made use of what was already in our hands—a piece of property—and continued operating faithfully as a congregation from our rented location.

This active waiting is what Isaiah described when he wrote, "Yet those who wait for the Lord will gain new strength" (Isaiah 40:31, NASB). Waiting here is much like what a waiter, or server, at a restaurant does. It speaks of an active, vibrant waiting—a waiting that can involve serving and giving. As we welcome delayed gratification and wait in faith for God to lift our limitations, we continue to make use of the things He has already given us. We serve Him, as a "server," anticipating His desires before we have to be told. This is faith-waiting. It anticipates, hopes, and expects. Contentment comes with this kind of waiting, for as we do it, we are resting in faith that God's plans will unfold in His timing, which is always perfect.

Believe in the Power of God's Plans

Welcoming delayed gratification becomes a little easier when we embrace the power of God's plans for our lives. We may not understand His plans; we may just catch glimpses of what God wants to accomplish through us on our journey with Him. But when we understand the power of having a purpose in God—when we consider that God made us because He wants to walk with us and show more of Himself to the world through us—then waiting becomes a little more natural, a little less of a strain.

We build contentment into our hearts as we remember there is a big picture—a path of life—and that prison is only one part of the journey. While we may not see how our brokenness, pain, or limiting circumstance could possibly fit into good plans, God sees our end from our beginning (Isaiah 46:10). Jesus said, "Do not let your heart be troubled; believe in God, believe also in Me" (John 14:1, NASB). As we set our hearts on believing God to fulfill His plans, just being with Him—the All-Sufficient One, the God who sees everything—brings comfort and rest.

GOING TO THE LIGHT

Living at the Next Level is a rich topographical experience. As the Israelites found true of the Promised Land, our friendship journey with God includes mountains and valleys, fertile plains and desert places. Up to now, we've focused on what seem like the desert places and valleys. But what of the mountains and fertile plains? We yearn for these—for change, good things, and fruitful times. Isn't this what we mean when we say we want to "see something" in life?

Often, to protect ourselves from disappointment, we give up our hope of ever experiencing the heights. We settle for just the experience of internal change in our heart, mind, and character, and relinquish our hope of seeing things change for us externally. And yet, external change is a part of our journey. Even as there are periods of limitation—seasons spent in prisons, ditches, and at dead-ends—so there are periods of release. We can learn to practice contentment in our prisons, learn to love God more deeply, and to rest in His love; but we also must remind ourselves that we are not necessarily serving a life sentence. God can break us out of limitations the moment He's ready, and if we're not careful, we will arrive at God's "Now" moment unprepared.

As we're about to see with Peter, when God says, "Now," He means, "Now." At the appointed time, God will shine a light into the darkness of our cell and tell us to get up. We need to be ready for that moment so we don't grope around, confused, when the light comes on: confused because we've resigned ourselves to the disappointments of prison, limitation, desert, and valley and forgotten that this leg of the journey is just that—a leg of the journey; only temporary.

Practicing contentment is one way we get ourselves prepared for the light. Another way is by going to the light we have available right here in our cell. I mean the light of God's Word. David wrote, "Your word is a lamp to my feet and a light to my path" (Psalm 119:105, NASB). Reading the Word and seeking God for understanding about your path may be a new experience for you, but this is the kind of light that must come on in your heart so you can break out at the Next Level. Your release is not going to happen through positive thinking. At this stage in the journey, we need to understand what God's Word says so we can come into agreement with it in preparation for our release.

Why not try going to the Word right now? You may find the Word challenging to understand. Maybe it would be helpful to look into some verses together here as a way to practice. One of my favorite books of the Bible is the Psalms. In the Psalms, we find every emotion of the heart confessed in familiar language. The Psalms—or songs— are earthy and real. They don't present a panacea for human struggle. They reveal real issues and challenges that several writers, including David, faced. The writers ask questions we can understand, like, "Why do wicked people prosper? Why do they always seem to get off scot-free?" Far from getting upset with these writers for being honest, God responds to them. When reading the Psalms, I feel released to express myself honestly to God too.

So what did one of the psalmists write when he was stuck in a place of limitation, fighting discouragement, struggling to keep himself out of frustration and renewed in hope? How did he attempt to take hold of contentment? Let's go to Psalm 42 (NASB).

It starts this way: "As the deer pants for the water brooks, so my soul pants for You, God" (v. 1). Here we have the psalmist expressing his first longing—his desire for God. The deer isn't just thirsty for water; it can't live without water. For us, our prison experience is often what surfaces our deepest thirst: a thirst for intimacy with God. Many times, the frustration we experience while walking through limitations is indicative of our longing for Him. Right from the start, the psalmist identifies the essential thing—his need for God, his heart for God's friendship—and expresses it.

Then, we read, "My tears have been my food day and night, while they say to me all day long, 'Where is your God?'" (v. 3). Here the writer is refusing to live in denial. Things are bad. He's crying day and night. His enemies are taunting him, mocking his relationship with a God who doesn't seem to be coming through for him; and the psalmist puts it out there. He's not afraid to identify what God already knows he's up against.

A few verses down, the writer makes a decision: "Hope in God, for I shall again praise Him for the help of His presence" (v. 5). Do you see how the writer's emotional journey in this psalm loosely tracks with our steps for embracing contentment? We look our limitations in the face. We acknowledge how bad they are, refusing to live in denial. Then, we make a decision: "Hope in God."

"For I shall again praise Him" speaks of delayed gratification. The psalmist is saying, "The time is coming. It may not be happening for me right now, but the day is going to come when I'm fully recovered and good things will happen for me again."

He writes, "Therefore I remember You from the land of the Jordan" (v. 6). Here some believe the psalmist is looking back to a time when God delivered him, standing on that memory as proof that there is hope for the future. He is practicing our second Next Level heart attitude—a heart of gratitude to God—giving thanks for what God has already done as a way to encourage himself. This action of the psalmist's heart speaks of his faith in the power of God's plans for him. The writer is affirming that what God did before He can do again.

At the end comes the psalmist's refrain—his decision—more strongly stated, as if from an encouraged heart: "Hope in God, for I shall yet praise Him, the help of my countenance and my God" (v. 11).

Looking into that psalm just encouraged my heart. Recognizing his own despair about his prison, the psalmist literally walked himself, line-by-line, into a determination to trust God and to hope for release from limitations. He prepared himself for change. We can do the same thing as we walk through the Word of God. We can encourage ourselves and dare, like the psalmist, to hope again. We can go to the light of the Word, anticipating the light of God's "Now" on our Next Level journey. Because the time for the light is at hand, we must make our hearts ready.

Mapping Your Next Level Leadership Journey

MILE MARKER: WHERE AM I ON THE JOURNEY?

Can you identify a few ways in which God may be making the limitations of your current leadership journey a designer prison for you?

_____

_____

_____

_____

What areas in your life that need instruction and growth are your current prison exposing?

_____

_____

_____

Begin to identify some of the ways in which God is reaching out to you, using your losses and limitations to build your friendship with Him. In what ways can these limitations motivate greater success?

_____

_____

_____

_____

CHARTING YOUR COURSE: FOCUSING
ON THE PATH AHEAD

The path ahead may remain limited as God develops you in this special place. Until things change, how can you change? I'm convinced that, as we change, everything around us will begin to adjust, as well. When you think of the four strategic steps I outlined, which resonates most with you and why?

Come out of Denial

_____

_____

_____

_____

Make a Decision

_____

_____

_____

_____

Welcome Delayed Gratification

_____

_____

_____

Believe in His Plans

_____

_____

_____

_____

LEADER'S PRAYER: ASKING FOR GUIDANCE

"Father, thank You for arranging my life so that I grow in love, authenticity, and depth. Continue to heal my heart, renew my mind, and make me strong in my love for You and Your plan. In Jesus' name, amen."

LEADER'S WORD: RECEIVING GUIDANCE FROM HIS WORD

"Though the Lord gave you adversity for food and suffering for drink, he will still be with you to teach you. You will see your teacher with your own eyes. Your own ears will hear him. Right behind you a voice will say, 'This is the way you should go,' whether to the right or to the left."
—Isaiah 30:20-21 (NLT)

PART 3

BREAKING OUT AT THE NEXT LEVEL

CHAPTER 6

WHO TURNED ON THE LIGHT?

P lease, Mom!" My room had just gone from a wonderful, relaxing darkness to the most annoying brilliance. Talk about your Grand Illumination! There I was, adrift in a temperate sea of sleep, having a sweet, vivid dream, when suddenly, this woman bent on dragging me out of the water and onto a scorching beach had barged into my room, as if she had the right, and flicked on the light.

Do you know what I did? If you guessed that I screamed at her to turn those lights off, then you have the wrong idea about my mother. When I was sixteen, she was just thirty-three, and as strong and quick as I was. She also had a feisty, go-getter, take-no-prisoners approach to life. At thirty, she had gone back to school for her nursing degree and even joined the basketball team at the school, playing with young women a decade her junior. So no, I didn't yell at her or give her any lip. I did what anyone with sense would've done: I woke up.

Peter's position in the wee hours before his trial was a bit more precarious. When we left him, he was sleeping in his cell, chained between two soldiers, while other guards kept watch. What happened next was about as shocking as it gets. Here's the rapid-fire description from Acts: "And behold, an angel of the Lord suddenly appeared and a light shone in the cell; and he struck Peter's side and woke him up" (Acts 12:7, NASB).

This was not Peter's mother hitting the light switch on the prison wall and slapping Peter out of his seat. This was an angel. Not an angel as in a little Sunday-school-drawing angel with little wings and a little halo. This was a terrifying apparition—a massive, heavenly being who could defeat armies of spiritual forces. When angels showed up in the Bible, there was a reason they often said to people, "Fear not."

In this case, the angel showed up with a heavenly light and struck—not slapped, but struck—Peter to jar him into wakefulness. I don't know about you, but if my mother was menacing enough to get me to wake up the minute that light came on in my bedroom, then I have a hard time imagining giving some lesser response to an angel. Peter might have been sleeping peacefully, or at least passively; maybe he had prepared his heart for death at the proceedings later that morning. A light-filled visitation may not have been the first thing on his list of likely happenings, but here it was—an angel, a blow to the side, and a heavenly light. His response was reasonable: he woke up.

The passage in Acts uses the word "suddenly." Suddenly, an angel appeared. Suddenly, a light shone in the cell. Suddenly, Peter, asleep between two guards, felt a sharp pain in his side. Our Next Level journey may include seasons of limitation, but it also includes seasons of release. While there is a place for "Wait" at the Next Level, there is also a place for "Suddenly." God can break us out of our tight, limiting place the moment He's ready: Suddenly. Without warning. When it seems least likely. Just like that, God appears at the door and, like my mother, turns on the light.

So what do you do when the light comes on in the middle of your night? You've fallen asleep in your prison, and suddenly, the light comes on. What do you do? May I suggest that you do what I did every morning of my young life when my mother stood at my bedroom door calling my name, and what Peter did when that angel showed up in the prison cell and smacked him? It's really quite simple: wake up.

RELEASE, PETER-STYLE

God uses the whole of our lives to bring maximum glory to Himself. The Bible says we were created for God's glory (Isaiah 43:6-7). Everything pertaining to us must showcase God's love, point the world in God's direction, and produce worship of Him. If you are experiencing a limitation in your life, then ultimately, God will use it somehow to bring Himself glory. If God is releasing you from that limitation—if He is saying "Now," if this is your "Suddenly" moment—then He is doing so because now your release will bring Him glory. It's all about Him. As Paul wrote, we are not our own (1 Corinthians 6:19).

Consider the context of Peter's imprisonment: James, Peter's fellow apostle and leader, has just been executed by Herod. Yet here is an angel showing up to break Peter out of prison so he can continue leading the church. James died, but Peter will be spared. Both men walked with Jesus. Both men loved and faithfully served God. Why did one die and the other live?

The answer comes down to God's plan and purpose, and His desire for glory. In James's case, martyrdom is what brought God glory. For Peter, God had different plans. Scripture tells us Peter's arrest and imprisonment took place "during the days of Unleavened Bread." In other words, it was during the week of Passover, the celebration marking the deliverance of the Israelites from slavery in Egypt (Acts 12:3). Passover is one of the most important celebrations in Jewish tradition. It was also the time of year when Jesus was crucified. Arresting a leader of Jesus' followers at Passover was nothing short of throwing down the gauntlet before God. And God was about to give an answer. At the appointed time, God would turn on a light and escort Peter out right under the noses of Herod's soldiers. Just as James's death glorified God, so in Peter's case would a miraculous, eleventh-hour release.

You may be able to identify both James and Peter in the story of your own life. Perhaps something in your past didn't work out as you'd planned, but because you trusted and worshipped God in the midst of loss and disappointment, He was glorified in your situation. This was your James. There are other things in your life, however, through which God plans to get glory another way. Now, it is not your letting go of a certain dream that will glorify God. This time, holding onto that dream until you "see something" is what will bring God glory. This is your Peter.

God is efficient. He gets maximum work out of our limitations, and then He moves us on: the prison sentence is over. When Peter's prison had served its purpose, the angel showed up. For you, too, if God finishes using your limitations, your release will come. Even the fact that God has you reading this book is an indication that your change may be at hand. We're not having this conversation just to keep you satisfied with the past, to keep you living in the past, or to cause you to limit your understanding of life to the past. We're having this conversation because the past was critical and necessary to bring you to today so that God could bring you out of limitations He has finished using and into another season of your journey in friendship with Him.

Don't let the enemy convince you that a bold, Peter-style release is not for you. Think about it: somewhere along the way, you've already experienced a prison break; somewhere in your personal history, you have a reference point. Maybe for years, you prayed about something and saw nothing happen; then, a time came when you prayed, and your circumstances suddenly changed. You said, "God, if you could do it that quickly, then why didn't it happen five years ago?" God didn't do it five years ago because it wasn't time. He was still working in your circumstances. He was still making your prison work for you. He was still getting glory in some way while you were in your limitations. But when the time came, He moved. He said, "Yes, that's over now. I'm moving you to another place." The light came on, the angel came in and struck you, and you woke up.

RAISING THE BAR

When we live in limitations for a long time, we can forget that God is supernatural. He lives inside of us, but He is the Creator of the universe, a holy God, who exists outside of time, space, and the other earthly limits that frame our lives. While God forms His nature in us, He is not one of "us." He is God, and we are His creation. He can do anything He chooses at any time.

We need to raise the bar on our expectations. A heart of expectancy toward God is the third Next Level heart attitude we must cultivate on our journey. When Moses questioned God's ability to feed the Israelites in the wilderness, God said, "Is the LORD's power too little?" (Numbers 11:23, NASB) God was challenging Moses to raise his expectations, and He challenges us to do the same.

Next Level Heart Attitudes
1. A Heart for Friendship with God
2. A Heart of Gratitude to God
3. A HEART OF EXPECTANCY TOWARD GOD
4. A Heart to Seek God

Expecting God is what it means to live in friendship with Him. The Bible says of Abraham that he "believed God...and he was called a friend of God" (James 2:23, NASB). When we believe God, we can walk with Him, learn to love Him, let down our guard with Him, and depend on Him—we can become intimate with One whom we expect to come through. Expectancy is a place of trust, and trust is the basis of friendship.

Our problem is that we give up on God too easily. To protect our hearts from frustration in difficult times, we often lower our expectations of God. We don't want to suffer any more disappointment, and we fear that, if we dare to hope for change, we are setting ourselves up to be hurt. So what do we do? We shut down hope. We shut down our dreams. We shut down our expectations. We tell ourselves not to believe that God can be God.

But if we stop believing God, then what can be said of the health of our friendship with Him? We already know the enemy is out to degrade our friendship with God. Satan's whole mission with Adam and Eve was to get them to separate from God and try to live independently of Him. When we stop ourselves from expecting God because we're afraid of disappointment or continued frustration, we play right into the devil's hand. Ceasing to believe God, we draw back from Him. We begin looking for ways to solve our problems ourselves. We wander off course. We end up more frustrated. We drift even farther.

Building ourselves up in our third Next Level heart attitude, a heart of expectancy toward God, is one way we protect our friendship with Him. As we expect our Friend to be true to His Word, we can release our frustration and experience the fulfillment of resting in Him and enjoying the gift of His love. Confidence in God is a shield for our friendship with Him. The Bible urges us in expectancy: "Let us hold fast the confession of our hope without wavering, for He who promised is faithful" (Hebrews 10:23, ESV).

WHITE NIGHTS

God can make the light come on even when, by all accounts, it should be dark. Several years ago, I traveled to Estonia to preach. Now a dynamic, burgeoning nation, Estonia was ruled for centuries by outside powers—most recently by the Soviet Union—until it regained its independence in 1991. When I arrived in 1995 and began to preach, I was told that the people, who had suffered greatly under Stalin, were more open to my message than they had been to the ministry of some other Westerners, simply because they related to the oppression in my African American background. They related to prison, limitations, darkness.

Oddly, though, the country at that time was unusually bright. I mean literally bright. We visited Estonia, located between Russia and the Baltic Sea, in the summer. It was late at night by the time we finally got settled in our accommodations, but when I pulled the curtain back in my room, I became disoriented—the sun was shining. Though I had heard it was the season for "White Nights," the time of year at that latitude when darkness never completely falls, I just couldn't register sunlight in the middle of the night.

When God turns on the light in our lives, we might experience what I did looking out the window in Estonia—disorientation, disbelief. We say, "But wait—it's supposed to be dark and the lights are on!" Even now, you may be thinking, *This is not a reasonable time for change.* But, actually, it is. There is a light coming on in your cell.

Based on your circumstances, it should be dark, but it is not—God is turning on the light. All the circumstances don't have to be right before God can move. Remember, He is not limited by your limitations. At the point when you expect to experience your deepest darkness, God can give you a White Night.

I saw it in Estonia—a country that had suffered oppression for generations but was emerging from its prison, a country both literally and figuratively in the middle of a White Night, an entire nation positioned right where Peter was in his cell when the angel of God suddenly appeared. In a place where, for years, it had been "dark," people were experiencing "Now." The light had come on. It was time to wake up.

DON'T MISS THE WAKE-UP CALL

When the light comes on, you must respond. Peter's trial and likely execution were only hours away. That prison was about to become a dangerous place for him. When the light came on, Peter had to wake up. God was saying, "Now! Right now!"

Our position, too, is critical. When God says, "Wake up," He isn't being nonchalant. God doesn't waste words. If He says, "Now," then He means "Now." Like Peter's prison, our place of limitation is about to become unproductive—and unsafe. If we're going to make a break, we can't miss the wake-up call. Think about what would have happened if Peter had given up on God and missed his wake-up call—we might be reading a different story. That angel struck Peter to wake Him up. God didn't want his leader missing the miraculous release.

God deals the same way with us. He will smack us if necessary so we don't miss our prison break. He'll bring us some telling circumstances, some blows to our situation, some indicators that let us know, "Okay, it's time to do something here." God understands how our hearts and minds work. He sees us fighting to embrace contentment in our prison, only to wind up back in a place of hopelessness. He sees our desire to believe and expect of Him, even as we sink back into fear. He sees our hearts curling up in the dark as we say, "I guess God doesn't really care about me." We need to thank God that He sends His angel to strike us—to cut through that despair, anxiety, and doubt.

If you had a mother like mine, bent on making sure you got up for school in the mornings, then you have a reference point for God's determination. Your mother might have started out sweetly: "Baby, honey, sweetheart, you need to wake up. Sweetie, it's time to wake up." But give her about two seconds, and she'd come back like that angel—flipping on the light, snatching off covers, smacking you on the legs. Maybe your mother even threw water on you! You would come to consciousness thinking something like, *Gosh, you'd guess the whole world depended on my waking up right this second. Can't I get five more minutes?*

But your mother, father, aunt, uncle, grandparent, or whoever woke you up knew something. He or she knew that five more minutes meant you might miss the bus. Missing the bus might have meant you missed the first bell. Missing the first bell might have meant that you didn't get the homework assignment. Missing the homework assignment might have meant failing the quiz. Failing the quiz might have meant performing poorly on the midterm. Performing poorly on the midterm might have meant blowing the final. Blowing the final might have meant not even making it out of your current grade. Not getting out of that grade might have discouraged you so badly that you didn't try for college or vocational school.

God is smarter than your mother, father, or guardian. He knows how significant this moment is, and if He's got to snatch the covers off you and make your little comfortable spot uncomfortable, then He'll do it so that you don't miss the assignment. Your situation may not appear critical to you, but some of the things you've been praying about, hoping for, and expecting from God are all connected to a decision you've got to make right now about responding to the light. When God turns on the light, you can't sleep on it. You can't play with it. You've got to wake up.

And waking up is not a group activity. When God turns the light on in your life, you may be the only one who sees it. Your friends may be oblivious to the light—and they should be. What God is doing in your life may not be their issue right now. There's no need to try to get them to believe it or see it. They can't.

That's why they're looking at you like you've lost your mind. You're the only one seeing the light and the angel because you are the one God is releasing. There comes a time when we must understand God's will for our lives and respond to the light for ourselves. When the light comes on, as much as it may shake you, irritate you, and throw you out of your comfort zone, please respond. You don't want to stay in the prison, do you? By all means, wake up!

WAKING UP FAITH

The Bible says, "We walk by faith, not by sight" (2 Corinthians 5:7, NASB). If we're going to follow God's instructions and walk out of our limitations, then when that angel shows up, we must wake up our faith. Jesus said, "Have faith in God" (Mark 11:22, NASB). Faith in God is trust in God. When we say that our third Next Level heart attitude—a heart of expectancy toward God—flows out of our trust in God, we are really saying that it flows out of our faith in Him. Our Next Level journey is a "faith walk."

Scripture calls faith "the substance of things hoped for, the evidence of things not seen" (Hebrews 11:1, NKJV). A few years ago, our church outgrew the warehouse we had converted into our headquarters. We were at capacity for three Sunday services, and we struggled to create enough space for children and youth. How would we accommodate the people we believed God wanted to send us in the future if we could hardly handle those who were already coming? We realized what we had to do: expand.

Deciding to expand didn't mean instantly ordering up a fleet of cranes, truckloads of materials, and a wrecking ball. It started with a call to an architect and a set of detailed plans. The things we hope for in life are like those plans; plans are your starting point, but they are not your ending point. If you pay an architect to draw up plans—and you can pay thousands of dollars just for the plans—then you don't just throw them in a drawer and leave them there. To make what's on the plans a reality, you must join faith to those plans. You must believe in the vision depicted by the plans and then, in faith, start hauling in the bricks and mortar. Faith is the substance of the hopes enshrined in those plans. By faith, the plans become a building that people can use.

That verse from Hebrews also calls faith the "evidence" of what we do not see. Let's say I have a prayer request—and I have many. I can't see or imagine how God is going to work things out. If I can't see how things are going to work out, what keeps me praying? What makes me go back to God and keep talking to Him? What keeps me praying—not for days, but for weeks, months, years, or even decades? If I've been praying for that long, but I don't see any outward results, what makes me continue? I continue to pray because I carry in my spirit evidence that God will fulfill His Word in my life. What is that evidence? It's faith.

But what if I don't feel like I have any faith to wake up? What if my limitations have just about squeezed all the faith out of me? Trust me, you've got some faith. The Bible says God gives everyone a "measure of faith" (Romans 12:3, NASB). That means we all arrive on this earth with some built-in faith. Besides, you use yours every day. In faith, a week before payday, you plan to go to the mall and buy those shoes. In faith, you plan to have dinner with a friend on Saturday night. Do you test your sofa before you throw yourself down on it? Not likely. You have faith that it will hold you—just as you have faith that your employer will write you a good paycheck and faith that your car will carry you safely to your friend's house for dinner. Before you start telling yourself that you don't have any faith left and that life has all but killed it, think again. God gave you the measure of faith before you got here, and that faith—however small—is still functioning.

Furthermore, the issue isn't *how much* faith you have. The issue is *what* or *whom* you put your faith in. If we were talking about a weak God, then you would need a lot of faith. But when you put your faith in a supernatural God, the Creator of heaven and earth, all you need is a little faith. Jesus said if you have faith "the size of a mustard seed"—the size of a seed that will fit beneath your fingernail—then you have enough faith to move a mountain (Matthew 17:20). If you will make the decision to wake up that faith and to place it in God, you will be able to do everything required to walk right out of your prison.

STAYING AWAKE

Once he got to Peter's prison cell, the angel didn't slap Peter awake just for kicks. Peter was stunned into wakefulness because the angel needed him to take care of a few things. Whisking an unconscious Peter out of the prison and back into the city was not in the angel's orders. Peter was going to participate in his own prison break. And guess what? So are we.

When the light comes on, we can't wake up, roll over, and hit the snooze button. Now that we've come to consciousness and awakened our faith, we must learn to keep that faith awake so we can keep step with God as He breaks us out of our limitations. How do we do that? The Bible says that "faith comes by hearing" the Word (Romans 10:17, NKJV). God has given us the measure of faith—we received it when we were born. Now, we maintain and add to our faith by interacting with God's Word.

Hearing isn't just a physical response. You can tell your son 20 times to take out the trash. He may hear your words every time, but if he doesn't get out of the chair, he hasn't truly heard you. The same difference applies to the way we hear (or don't hear) God's Word. Hearing the Word means more than picking up with your ears what is being said. Sitting through a church service doesn't guarantee you've heard the Word. Hearing means receiving the Word into your spirit, accepting it as true, and preparing yourself to act accordingly (James 1:22-25).

To build up your faith—to keep it awake—you need to take in the Word of God daily. You need to read it, listen to it, respond to it, memorize it, and let God develop a dialogue with you through His Word. You not only add to your faith this way; you also cultivate that first Next Level heart attitude, a heart for friendship with God. Engaging with His Word, you learn to hear God's voice and understand His heart. By the time you get to a worship service at church, you should be so deep into God's Word that what you hear from the preacher or minister becomes an extension of your ongoing dialogue with God. You think, *Yes, Lord, I was just asking You that question last week*, and *Yes! That passage confused me last month, but now I understand. Now I see what You're saying to me.*

On the flip side, just as we build up our faith by taking the Word into our hearts, we can also diminish our faith based on what we "feed" our hearts and minds. Some of us are filling our spirits constantly with the kinds of words that leave our faith malnourished. Just consider some of the music we consume. It may be "just music" to us, but those same lyrics can shape or influence the way we respond when we find ourselves in challenging situations. We absorb so many words that run counter to God's Word, it's no wonder we can't love right, live right, or respond to the angel sent to break us out of our limitations. We must become fierce in faith and say, "I'm going to be guarded about what goes into my heart. I'm going to fill my head and my spirit every day with the Word of God. And I'm going to keep my faith awake."

THE LIGHT OF THE WORD

David called God's Word "a lamp to my feet and a light to my path" (Psalm 119:105, NASB). We've talked about going to the Word as a way of preparing our hearts for our "Suddenly" moment. We've talked about spending time in the Word in order to build up our faith and deepen our friendship with God. Well, guess what? That light coming on in our cell? That, too, is God's Word. It is God's "Now"—His creative, life-giving Word spoken into our situation to bring change.

The Bible says that by the Word of God everything was created (Hebrews 11:3). In Genesis, we read, "God said, 'Let there be light'; and there was light" (Genesis 1:3, NASB). Light was created—the light came on—because God spoke it into being. So it is in our lives right now. God has spoken "Now" into our prison. The light has come on. The Word has been released. Change has been activated. Something is happening, and if we fail to understand the importance of the moment, we might find ourselves hiding under the covers in fear.

As adverse as the light can seem when someone turns it on in your face, the light of God's Word is what you need. Some of the things God may say to you—some of the commands He gives—may not be agreeable at first; however, the light of the Word coming on in your life, even as it strengthens your faith, will also give you clarity about your journey. The Word is a lamp to our feet—it shows us where we are. I may not have it all together but, because God's Word is a lamp to my feet, I see where I am—where I've grown and where I need to grow. Then, the Word is a light to my path—it shows me where God is taking me from here. Even though I may stumble and my feet may get a little crazy, in the light of the Word, I can see the path of life stretching out in front of me.

Consider that—right now—while you sit in your cell, stunned by the light, your path of life is opening to you. You are not being ripped from a quasi-comfortable sleep in a dark, heavily guarded prison. You are being awakened by God to the next phase of your journey with Him. God has caused those weeks, months, or years of hard time in limitations to strengthen you, transform you, and bring you closer to Him in friendship. You've learned how to walk in gratitude to God. You've begun to build up a heart of expectation about what He can do. Now, the Lord's angel has burst into your cell, and your faith is awake—not momentarily awake, but awake for real. This is the time to turn up the volume on your expectations! Keep those eyes and ears open. Keep that third Next Level heart attitude, a heart of expectancy toward God, alive. God is about to start giving instructions, and He needs your undivided attention.

Mapping Your Next Level Leadership Journey

MILE MARKER: WHERE AM I ON THE JOURNEY?

Where in your leadership journey have you given up on the miracle?

_____

_____

_____

_____

Where have you decided that God is not coming through this time?

_____

_____

_____

_____

Peter walked in the third Next Level heart attitude—a heart of expectancy toward God. Are you ready to become expectant again?

_____

_____

_____

_____

CHARTING YOUR COURSE: FOCUSING
ON THE PATH AHEAD

Make a decision to be an authentic leader—one who anticipates God moving in unexpected ways. Be the leader who constantly turns on the light of the Word so that it can penetrate deeply into the prison. Begin asking God to awaken your hunger for the truth of His Word, and expect to understand His working your life.

LEADER'S PRAYER: ASKING FOR GUIDANCE

"Lord, I am convinced that You still have plans for me. Reveal Yourself to me through the light of Your Word. Let the revelation of Your truth wake me up in my place of limitation. I want to see what I've never seen before. In Jesus' name, amen."

LEADER'S WORD: RECEIVING
GUIDANCE FROM HIS WORD

"*Your word is a lamp to guide my feet and a light for my path.*"
—*Psalm 119:105 (NLT)*

CHAPTER 7

GET UP QUICKLY

G et up quickly, Peter!"

Was I dreaming? It seemed like a vision—the dark cell illuminated by an otherworldly light; the towering figure, like that of a man, wrapped in a pillar of light. *A dream*, I thought. *A strange, heavenly dream.*

Then, the man in the light lunged toward me, leaving a sharp pain in my side and the words, "Get up quickly!" ringing in my ears. My side began to throb. My vision seemed to blur. Suddenly, I saw a scene from my past. A memory? Yes. I saw light dancing over a pool and could hear the pained murmur of sick people. We were near the Sheep Gate at the healing pool. I could picture it all, and in my mind, I heard the Teacher's voice.

"Get up!"

Several feet from where the rest of us stood, Jesus squatted next to a man and spoke forcefully. The man had been minding his own business. He was stretched out on his mat near the pool like so many others when Jesus approached.

I thought, *What do these people do all day while they wait for their miracle, for the angel they believe will stir up the waters? So many sick people. Waiting day after day. What do they do? How do they stand it— the waiting?* I didn't know. But I guessed they were likely not ready for Jesus and the drama that always unfolded wherever He went.

We hung back and watched the Teacher's interaction with the man. We were getting used to this now—following the Teacher, standing by during His encounters with the sick, the poor, the religious leaders. We'd seen Him angry, turning over tables in the temple. We'd seen Him tender, speaking gently to a Samaritan woman at Jacob's well. Here, at the pool of Bethesda in Jerusalem, speaking to the man on his mat, Jesus seemed a little of both: angry—or was it just firm?—and tender. Intense *and* kind.

Later, we learned that the man had been sick for 38 years. 38 years! A lifetime of waiting. And there, Jesus had walked right up to him and asked the man, as only Jesus could, what appeared to be the most ludicrous question: "Do you want to get well?"

Who but the Master would dare ask such a thing? What did He expect the man to say? "No, I like being in this condition, ill for almost 40 years!" I could never get used to the Teacher's disarming approach. He would either ask an impossible question or give an unthinkable command. Today would be no different.

Looking on, we couldn't hear the man's response, but it must have been the wrong one, because immediately, the Teacher yelled out, "Get up! Pick that bed up and walk!"

Here we go again, I thought. It was the Sabbath, and the critics would have a field day: "Your Master breaks the laws of the Sabbath. Your Master is an egomaniac." Of course, sometimes, we too wondered about Him—He was different. But, as in all the other instances of miracles worked by the Master, the one thing the critics couldn't do was deny the obvious. As soon as Jesus yelled, "Get up!" the man immediately got up, picked up his mat, and began to walk.

Once the man started walking, it clicked; I understood what Jesus had done. With His words, He had cut right through the man's condition—through his sickness, his resignation, the 38 years—and awakened the man's faith to believe for what surely seemed impossible. What sounded like an uncaring command was actually a unique display of love. The man was doomed to die waiting by that water unless Someone with an authoritative Word ordered him to do what he did not feel capable of doing. That was Jesus' way—to press people to do what they could not do on their own. The man just had to believe and then try. When he did, the power of heaven came on him to help—to help him get up. "Get up!"

"Get up!" The light again—the man in the light. Moving toward me. My chains shaking. The cold weight of them on my arms and ankles. The pain in my side. The damp air in the cell. Yes. The cell. I was still in the cell.

"Quickly!" the Light-Man said, his words ringing. "Get up quickly!"

TAKING RESPONSIBILITY

For those of us who are parents—and, really, anyone can relate to this, because we've all been children—we've probably said 100 times things like, "If you want to do this, you're going to have to be more responsible. If you want a car, you have to prove you can be responsible with it. If you want those sneakers, you must show me you can take care of your possessions."

Have you ever noticed, too, the way parents can bring everything back to cleaning up your room? "If you want a new outfit, you're going to have to clean up your room. If you want to go to college, I want to see you clean up your room. You want to go to the movies with your friends? Clean up your room." All kinds of privileges and opportunities can hinge on that one responsibility. If you can't clean up your room, you can't go anywhere or do anything.

What are parents really getting at when we place these kinds of conditions on our children? We're saying that, while there are many good things our kids desire—and while we, too, desire good things for our kids—unless our kids learn to handle themselves responsibly, those good things could very well crush them. God deals with us in the same way: He knows that a blessing can quickly become a curse if we don't know how to handle it properly.

Can you remember a time in your life when you wanted something, maybe a relationship—wanted it desperately—but then, after you got it, you realized you weren't ready—it ended up being something that pulled you down rather than lifted you up? Have you ever pressed God for something—pushed and pushed—and, when He finally gave you what you wanted, you started asking about the return policy? "God, do I have to pay shipping and handling on this? Can't I just give it back to You ... now?"

The truth is that we really don't know what's best for us all the time. We may pray, "God, I want this right now." And God may release it to us just to let us experience what a blessing given prematurely feels like. On the other hand, if He sees we're not ready, He may withhold it. Anyone who's lived for just a little while knows to thank God for withholding what we cannot handle—that withholding is an act of love. While God is holding back the blessing, He is teaching us responsibility. For in order to flourish in the coming phase of our Next Level journey, we've got to be men and women who can take responsibility, carefully following God's instructions, even when His instructions don't make sense.

After the angel showed up in Herod's prison and awakened Peter, the angel gave Peter several directives. The first was, "Get up quickly." Later, we'll see why such a seemingly simple command made no sense in Peter's situation; regardless, "Get up!" was what God, through the angel, told Peter to do. You see, God was doing His part in the prison break. The angel showing up with a light in the prison was a miracle; that angel walked through walls and turned off the guards' abilities to perceive him. But while God moved supernaturally to ensure Peter's rescue, He also required Peter to do a couple of things—to take responsibility and do his part.

God is more than willing to move supernaturally in your life. He turns on the light; He sends you His angel, His power, His help. But if you do not take responsibility for your part—the "Get up!" part—you can miss out on the beautiful plan of God for that moment. You'll have a testimony of God doing something miraculous for you, but then, you'll have to answer the question, "What did I do in response to the miracle?" The angel showing up is nice. Peter could've written a nice book about the angel showing up in his cell. But what would it have mattered if Peter had been escorted out to trial by some of those guards the next day because he failed to respond to the angel's commands? God certainly could've found another way to rescue His leader, or found another person to lead in Peter's place; but think of the release God had arranged that night in the prison—the release Peter would have missed!

If God steps into your situation and performs a miracle, often, in order for the miracle to fulfill what it was sent to do, you must respond. The miracle doesn't come simply to make you feel good for a few minutes; it comes to bring you into a life you never could have lived were it not for God. It comes so you can say "goodbye" to hopelessness, lack, and a lifestyle of failure and "hello" to joy, healthy relationships, peace, and wholeness. The miracle comes to move you out of the desert and into the fertile plain, out of the prison and into the city, out of one phase of your Next Level journey and into another. The miracle comes to move you. So when the angel shows up in Peter's cell, the very first words out of his mouth are these: "Get up quickly!"

SEEING SOMETHING

To this point in the book, we've spent our time realigning our thinking about God and life, making internal issues our primary focus. We've come to understand, first, that we were made for friendship with God. Our relationship with God is the ultimate gift—greater than any external, earthly blessing we could ever imagine. God said to Abraham, "I am ... your exceedingly great reward" (Genesis 15:1, NKJV). Friendship with God, we understand, *is* the Next Level.

Friendship with God is also our priority. Loving God is the first great commandment, and a heart for God's friendship is the first Next Level heart attitude we give ourselves to developing (Mark 12:28-30). Paul wrote that his heart's desire was to know God (Philippians 3:8-11). This must be our first desire, too. Fulfillment comes in knowing and loving God—that is what living at the Next Level is all about.

We've also learned to maintain and express gratitude to God—our second Next Level heart attitude. God has been faithful to us, taking care of us in our limitations, even when we did not know or welcome Him. As we thank God for what He has already done, we build up our ability to trust Him with our present and our future. We learn to let go of frustration and rest in Him. Our friendship with God deepens and, in a posture of gratitude, we gain a greater sense of awe about the One who desires to be our Friend—the Creator, the All-Sufficient One, the One who calls Himself "I AM" (Exodus 3:14).

We've recognized, too, that we can expect God to honor His Word in our lives. Our expectation of God flows out of our trust in God— our faith—which is the basis of our friendship with Him. As we cultivate our third Next Level heart attitude, a heart of expectancy toward God, we protect that friendship. When we believe God, placing our expectation in Him, we are better able to rest in Him and stay connected. We can transform our frustration into fulfillment as we trust our Friend with everything that concerns us and learn to enjoy the gift of loving Him every day.

Next Level Heart Attitudes
1.   A Heart for Friendship with God
2.   A Heart of Gratitude to God
3.   A Heart of Expectancy Toward God
4. A HEART TO SEEK GOD

All of these lessons touch us at the heart level—they are heart attitudes. Prioritizing our friendship with God, learning to live in gratitude to God, cultivating our expectation of God—these constitute internal adjustments that we make as we learn how to live at the Next Level. But there is more to Next Level living than internal growth. Internal adjustments are also the beginning of external adjustments! The Bible says that as a man "thinks in his heart, so is he" (Proverbs 23:7, NKJV). As we align our thoughts and attitudes with God's, we prepare ourselves for the external changes He wants to make in our lives.

God does want us to "see something." He is madly in love with us, and His love demands to be demonstrated. God wants us to experience change in our hearts, but He also wants that heart change to work itself out in our lives. He wants His will for us to come to pass both in the internals and the externals. Think about Peter. The angel showed up with a light, struck Peter on the side, and woke him up. But there was more—much more—God planned to do for Peter; and the same is true for you and me. God wakes us up spiritually, but our waking up isn't the end of change—it is just the beginning. God says, "I don't want you to be awake in your faith only. It's not just about your heart being right toward Me. I also want your life to be changed. I want your body and mind to be whole. I want chaos in your life to be straightened out. I want your relationships to be healthy. I don't want you just to wake up—I want you to *get up*!"

INTERNALS AND EXTERNALS

If we look at Scripture, we discover that "seeing something" is a vital part of our faith walk with God. We can't even discuss faith in a complete way without talking about both internals and externals. The Bible says, "And without faith it is impossible to please Him, for the one who comes to God must believe that He exists, and that He proves to be One who rewards those who seek Him" (Hebrews 11:6, NASB). In other words, the seeker of God—the one going after the internals—must also believe that God is a rewarder...and reward can involve externals. We may not see all of our dreams fulfilled, but the man or woman of faith must expect to see something—must believe that God is a rewarder— or fail to please Him.

Proverbs tells us, "Hope deferred makes the heart sick, but when the desire comes, it is a tree of life" (Proverbs 13:12, NKJV). That is a verse about internals and externals. If God puts a hope in our hearts, then we can believe that, in some way, He plans to make it a tree of life for us. The internal hope by itself is incomplete; the external achievement by itself is both incomplete and shallow. On our Next Level journey—our faith walk with God—we need to experience both.

Maybe you've grown so accustomed to your prison that you've convinced yourself external change is not as important as you once believed. Internal, heart-level growth is what matters, you've determined, and you've resigned yourself to expecting only that. But if internal change is all we can count on, then why is it that, even when our priorities are properly aligned—even when we put heart issues and our friendship with God first—we still long for external change? The answer is that external change is part of God's plan, too. Our relationship with God is our first priority, but external issues do matter. They matter to us and they matter to God, because He loves us.

On the other hand, maybe you are someone who has focused on your external circumstances for so long, and with such intensity, that the internal issues seem less significant. Frustration with life has taken center stage. You can't seem to make the changes you want to make. You're constantly aware of your chains. You keep rattling them, but they won't break—you can't get loose. That is because God has wanted to teach you how to make internal issues your first priority. He knows that, if you fail to embrace your friendship with Him and adjust your thinking in certain areas, then even in external success, you will live an unfulfilled life, never becoming what you were ultimately created to be—His intimate friend. God has always wanted to free you, but you will need to address your issues in accordance with His priorities.

What if I fail in the internal process? What if I can't get these heart attitudes to register inside? What if I can't overcome my own laziness or lack of desire for God or frustration with my external circumstances? What if I can't seem to let go of what *I* want and want what *God* wants? What if I'm incapable of settling down and enjoying the journey? Does this mean I miss out on God's plans for my life? I'm so weak in my heart. Is it all up to me?

Our growth in God is not all up to us. Our part is deciding to walk with God through the process of growth. God will empower us in that process, but we must decide—we must be willing—and commit to following Him. What if our decision is mixed with doubt? Well, Jesus made allowance for doubt. When the father of a boy harassed by an evil spirit came to Jesus begging, "If You can do anything, take pity on us and help us!" Jesus said to him, "'If You can?' All things are possible for the one who believes" (Mark 9:22-23, NASB). What the father of the boy said next reveals the internal conflict and inadequacy we so often feel: he said, "I do believe; help my unbelief" (Mark 9:24). The man was not contradicting himself. He was deciding to place his faith in Jesus while, at the same time, recognizing the doubt in his heart. What did Jesus do? He looked right through the doubt, acknowledged the man's decision to believe, and validated it. How? By healing the man's son. By working in the externals of the man's life.

God can do the same for you. The light has come on in your cell. The angel has struck you. You're finally awake, but you're still in your chains. Now, God is bringing you an authoritative Word—the same Word Jesus brought to the man who was sick at the healing pool for 38 years. It's a Word to let you know that He sees your heart. He sees your desire to follow Him. He sees through the doubt, selfishness, and failure. He sees you in your struggle, and He wants to free you. Just as you engaged your faith and decided to believe that God could help you make the internal adjustments in your heart, now you must make another decision—this one related to externals. When the

Word comes, will you do as the sick man did? Will you do as Peter did? Will you get up?

DO WHAT YOU CANNOT DO

I don't know about you, but it appeals to my curiosity that the very first thing the angel told Peter to do was something Peter could not do. "Get up!" may sound like a simple command, but for someone in Peter's position, getting up was not only difficult—it was impossible. Peter was still chained between two guards. Those chains were there to keep Peter from getting up. If Peter wanted to get up in the night, he would have to ask those two guards for permission.

Somehow, Peter must've known what the angel meant when he said, "Get up quickly." The angel was not telling Peter to shake one of the guards and ask to go free; he was telling Peter to get up on his own, chains and all. Notice that Peter did not seem offended by the command. He never even answered the angel. He didn't say, "Why are you doing this to me? How can you demand that? Don't you see that I'm chained to these guards?" Peter had walked with Jesus for three to three-and-a-half years of Jesus' ministry. Peter was there at the healing pool when Jesus told the man who had been sick for 38 years to get up and walk. "Get up" was a command familiar to Peter. When he heard the angel say it, Peter was simply hearing the words of his Lord again.

But back to the command itself. "Get up" was nevertheless impossible. How was Peter to do it? Let me stop here and say this: breaking out at the Next Level will often begin with God asking you to do something you cannot do on your own. God will challenge you to step out in faith—in the very faith you have awakened and built up— and do something that, by yourself, you have no capacity to do. Many of us shrink back when such a command is given. God tells us to "Get up quickly," and, rather than step out and try, we start looking at our chains, our guards, and our restrictive environment. We say, "God, I can't do it. I can't do what You're asking me to do."

Can you relate to this scenario? Have you ever felt God drawing you to do something but then failed to believe you could do it? You didn't have the energy to get up. You couldn't move. It was as if your past experiences had left you so numb or stunned that you couldn't even respond to God. You heard the Word; you knew God wanted to break you out of your limitations; but somewhere in your heart, you said, "I just can't do this, Lord."

I know how that feels, and I agree with you. You are right. You can't do this. You can't get up when you're chained down. The good news is that God is not instructing you to get up in your own strength. God is saying, "I just need you to come into agreement with Me. I need you to link up your will with My will and say 'yes' to what I'm asking of you. If you will just say 'yes' to 'Get up,' then I will get you up Myself."

In the face of an impossible command, rather than sink deeper into frustration, we must engage our faith. Like the father of the boy harassed by an evil spirit, we make the decision: "Lord, I believe. Help my unbelief!" We say, "Lord, I can't get up on my own, but I believe You can get me up!" Obedience is always possible. When God gives a command, He has already determined to remove whatever might be in our way and help us obey Him. God is for us—He wants us to make it.

Be mindful that, in order to take a stance of faith like this in your heart, you must resist the discouraging voices. Go back to what we learned about the guards. Those guards around you—guards of depression, discouragement, failure, and drama—are not just standing there; they're trying to keep you down. Every time you try to move, one of your guards will say, "Where are you going?" and, "What do you think you're doing?" and, "So you think you're getting up? You think you're getting out of here? You're not getting out. We've got you locked up here forever."

Remember what we said about those guards: they are the signs of our potential. Herod probably had more faith in Peter's potential than Peter himself. Don't you know your enemy sees the potential in your life? Those guards are not an indication that you can't get up. They're the proof that you can! Listen: the enemy believes in you. He has put all kinds of obstacles around you because he knows that, if you ever get your thinking right—if you ever begin to embrace the Word of God, if you ever begin to believe what the Word says about you—then there is no prison, no number of guards, that can hold you back from walking out God's plans for your life. With those kinds of stakes, of course, the enemy is doing everything he can to make you think you can't get up.

Fair enough. But why the impossible command? The angel enters the prison, shines a light, and says to Peter, "Get up. Do what you cannot do. Do what you're not capable of doing. Do what you lack the strength to do." Why give Peter instruction that is unfeasible? Is it just a faith test? Or consider Jesus with the man who was sick for 38 years. Why would Jesus tell an infirm man to get up and walk? The man had been sick for nearly four decades. Why ask him to do what he clearly couldn't do?

The answer is that Jesus sees what we cannot see. When Jesus sends a Word into your life, He isn't looking at your current circumstances or restrictions. He already sees you free, walking, and whole. He isn't seeing your chains. When God sent the angel to Peter, God didn't tell the angel, "Go down and inspect Peter's chains. Go see how strong they are. Would you find out whether they're made of titanium or iron? Please spend some time investigating those chains." No. God wasn't even seeing Peter in those chains; the chains were a nonissue. God simply sent the angel to get Peter out of prison; and since the angel was operating according to the Word of God, none of the intervening circumstances between Peter's bondage and his freedom made any difference. When the angel looked at Peter, all he saw was a man out of prison—the Word of God accomplished.

The same is true for you. God doesn't look at you and see chains. You can rattle your chains if you want; but when God looks at you, He sees a free man or woman. By telling you to get up, God is simply awakening His purpose and desire for your life. If, in your heart, you can agree with Him—if you can engage your faith and say "yes"— then His Word will cut right through your condition, your chains, and your 38 years, and empower you to do what He's asking.

THE CHAINS FELL OFF

God is at work in our lives—we need to catch it. This is not a game. This is not a dress rehearsal. This is the real thing. We are living at the Next Level, and God has plans for us. Experiencing those plans is not a passive exercise. God does His part but, as we are learning, we must do ours. We draw near to God, engage with Him, acknowledge where we are on the journey, recognize when it is time to break out, and ask ourselves, "What is my responsibility? How do I respond to the Word that God is sending me?"

At the Next Level, I trust God to do His part, and I decide to do mine, having the confidence to attempt it because I know my Friend is alongside to help. Do you know what happened when Peter decided to get up? This is not a trick question. Once the angel said to Peter, "Get up quickly," we read, simply, "And his chains fell off his hands" (Acts 12:7, NASB). His chains fell off!

Obedience may feel like a risk, but God always makes obedience possible. Maybe Peter said, "You know what? I know I can't get up, and I don't know why this angel is asking me to do it; but I don't want to die tomorrow, so I might as well take my chances. I might as well try." Maybe he engaged his quadriceps and leaned forward to get his footing. Maybe then he discovered that God had already touched the chains.

You might be in Peter's position right now: you're wondering whether you should take the risk and try. I want to encourage you— take a chance with God. You've taken a chance with everybody else. You've trusted other people, and they've let you down. You might as well believe God for a few minutes. So what if you lack the capacity to make everything happen? You have the capacity to get started. When God says, "Get up," you can decide you're going to try. As you decide to obey, God will do what you're not able to do. If you will say "yes" to His Word, He will empower you. He will deal with your chains.

Let's make the decision now: "God, I'm going to do what You tell me to do, say what You tell me to say, go where You tell me to go, and live as You tell me to live." God will respond to that decision. We may fail miserably in our efforts to obey Him, but the decision to obey *in spite of* our confusing emotions and failed attempts is pleasing to God. He is looking at our hearts.

I've learned this lesson in my own life. For years, I believed that, if I failed to obey God on every point, He would no longer be willing to work through me. If I blew it in my actions and made a mess out of trying to get up, I feared God would change His mind about His plans for my life. But after watching myself stumble for a while and seeing God stick with me and use my life for good, I began to understand what He was really after: my heart, my decision to trust Him, my desire to obey and get up. I saw that, if I kept my heart right before God—if loving Him remained my first heart attitude—then, in time, my chains would fall off. God would empower me in my weakness, and I would be able to do what He asked.

Whatever your issue—that nemesis issue that keeps you struggling to fulfill the acts of obedience God has set before you—understand that God loves you. He is for you. He wants you to be free. If your heart's decision is to obey Him, to get up quickly, and to follow His instructions, then even though you may have unbelief mixed in with your faith, those chains will fall off, and you will be able to obey.

QUICKLY

We've already discussed the urgency of God's wake-up call—it is critical we don't miss it. But lest we have any doubts about our need to move when God says to move, here it is in black-and-white. The angel did not say to Peter, "Get up when you feel like it. Get up when you feel led by the Spirit. Get up after you receive seven confirmations and eight prophetic words." No, no. The angel said, "Get up quickly." Right now. In a hurry. It's time to go!

The angel knew Peter only had a set number of hours before his public hearing. Only God knows what you may be facing. If you play around, you may wind up somewhere you don't want to be; so when God tells you it's time to break out, do not hesitate to do what He says—get up quickly. God will go to great lengths to get through to you, but you must respond. He may be grabbing you right now, saying, "It's time to go. You've got to move now. I've called you. I've spoken to you. Acknowledge what I'm telling you, and move!"

If God tells you to get out of the relationship, then you've got to stop emailing. If God tells you to make the call, then you must make the call. If He shuts something down in your life, let it go. Stop trying to bring it back. Quit propping it up and putting it on life support. When God says, "Get up quickly," He is saying, "I'm finished with that now. It may have brought you this far on your journey, but it won't take you any farther." There is a time in life for making your connecting flight. If God says, "Enough is enough," you must respond immediately. You have to get off the plane if you want to make your connection.

LET'S TRY AGAIN

I just want to say, "You can do it." You can try. You can move when God sends the Word. Maybe you've been reading along and you're beginning to understand some things about God, but you still struggle with making the decision to try. Maybe God is saying, "Get up quickly," in some area of your life, and you're afraid of risking it. You're afraid of one more disappointment. What if it doesn't work? You've been knocked down so many times you're not sure God even loves you, much less that He wants to remove your chains. You just can't see what God sees when He looks at you—a free man or woman. You can't even imagine it.

When Jesus asked the man who was sick for 38 years if he wanted to be well, the man responded by giving excuses as to why he had not yet made it down to the healing pool. He didn't even answer Jesus' question. Maybe he didn't have the strength left to even desire healing. Maybe he had buried his own dream. And yet, when Jesus released the Word—"Get up!"—the man found the willingness to try again. Scripture reads, "Immediately the man became well, and picked up his pallet and began to walk" (John 5:9, NASB). Immediately, the chains of sickness fell off, and the man responded. The Word of God mixed with the man's small faith and willingness to try is what freed him. It is what freed Peter. And it can free you.

Though you are not Peter, and though you haven't encountered Jesus in the flesh like the man at the healing pool, you may have experienced at least one situation in life that looked doomed or impossible. Still, things worked out. Maybe you believed that luck, coincidence, or fate was behind the success of your situation. On the other hand, maybe it was the Lord saying, "Get up quickly." You may not have seen God behind your circumstances at the time, but somehow, in your desperation, you made the decision to try to get up, and things worked out.

May I suggest that what happened once can happen again? I'm not asking you to climb Mount Everest. I'm just encouraging you: why not try again? The light has come on. Your faith is awake. You can't go back to sleep. You'll never be happy if you stay chained like this in a confined place, surrounded by guards. Your hope for something better in life is still burning—even if faintly. You've seen things go your way before. If God is saying, "Get up quickly," why not just try and see what happens? You can do it. You can make that decision to try.

Mapping Your Next Level Leadership Journey

MILE MARKER: WHERE AM I ON THE JOURNEY?

Leaders are often asked to "pivot" and move in a new direction—and to do it "quickly!" In what areas of your leadership journey do you sense a need to move quickly?

_____

_____

_____

_____

Amazingly, we wait on God in our limitations and, when He shows up, things move more quickly than we were prepared for. Peter's leadership is about to shift in influence and scope. Where do you see the potential for the same in your own sphere of influence?

_____

_____

_____

_____

CHARTING YOUR COURSE: FOCUSING ON THE PATH AHEAD

You have given some significant time and energy to deepening your friendship with God over the past few weeks. These times often precede new opportunities to lead and to serve. Spend some time surveying the leadership landscape of your life, and write down what you're seeing. Talk with your peers and find out what they are hearing at this time. Share your thoughts with others, as well. A collaborative effort can spur new thinking and fulfillment.

LEADER'S PRAYER: ASKING FOR GUIDANCE

"Lord, thank You for making internal and external changes in my life and leadership process. As You bring about change, help me to do my part. I believe that, whenever You give me a command, You will provide everything I need to fulfill Your requirements. With Your help, Lord, I will stand and walk and declare and serve, knowing You will empower me to do so. Make me ready for the next phase of my journey and lead me by Your Spirit. In Jesus' name, amen."

LEADER'S WORD: RECEIVING GUIDANCE FROM HIS WORD

"When Jesus saw him lying there, and knew that he had already been a long time in that condition, He said to him, 'Do you wish to get well?' The sick man answered Him, 'Sir, I have no man to put me into the pool when the water is stirred up, but while I am coming, another steps down before me.' Jesus said to him, 'Get up, pick up your pallet and walk.'"
—John 5:6-8 (NASB)

CHAPTER 8

GET DRESSED

Hyderabad-Secunderabad, India. December 2005. The close of a three-night Christmas celebration at Secunderabad's Bison Polo Grounds, a huge open space that was now a sea of faces—tens of thousands. Men, some in Western-style dress, and women, dressed in colorful winter saris and wraps, sat attentively with their children in tight rows on the ground as I stood on the stage next to the translator and preached.

On this night, I was preaching about the "Unknown God," wording the apostle Paul took from an Athenian altar, and about how we could know this God and become His friend (Acts 17:16-34). I would speak a phrase through the microphone and wait for the translation. Another phrase. Wait. Translation. I had come to love this process of communicating. It took on a wonderful rhythm all its own, though preaching this way, by speaking and waiting, did require preparation.

This was our last night in India—the climactic end to a trip that included ministry to church leaders, a village church dedication, and citywide Christmas events in two cities. It was my second trip to the subcontinent. My love for the Indian people had drawn me back. I had preached day and night and, here at the end, on this third night at the Polo Grounds, I could sense God's love for the people and what I believed was His desire to free them from issues and hurts that were keeping them down.

To close out the meetings, our host had staged a finale in celebration of Jesus' birth that included the release of thousands of helium balloons. Early in the evening, I had watched as the balloons were distributed by volunteers climbing and stretching over the mass of seated people. Then, at the appointed time, our host handed me an enormous colorful bunch to release on the count of three. We all counted, the thousands of us, and on three, as the band began to play a Christmas carol, we all let go. A whole field of balloons rose into the night sky, drifting, drifting from view.

Standing there on the platform, marveling in that atmosphere of celebration, I imagined the balloons as lives taking off, dreams flying high, and our prayers rising to God. Watching the sea of raised faces, the movement of hands and colorful saris, I suddenly became aware. Aware of what I believed was a longing in the people to rise, as the balloons were rising, above their limitations. Aware of the sacrifice Jesus made so that people from America to India and beyond could be free. Aware that my extensive preparation for this trip—even my lifetime of preparation—had been critical in helping me to do what God had asked of me here: to point others toward friendship with Him.

In the midst of the singing and dancing, in the clamor of thousands of voices, as balloons of all colors rose and disappeared, I knew that, through my own limitations, God had equipped me for this moment. He had changed me, awakened me, helped me get up, and helped me get ready to love people whom I'd never seen—and to invite them on the journey of a lifetime.

GETTING READY

If you are going to take a journey anywhere, you must take the time to get ready. Our months of preparation for India included things like prayer, logistics coordinating, team development, applications for visas and passports, the dispensing of shots and medications, and financial planning. Our ministry leaders from India gave us advice: take your malaria medicine. Stay away from tap water. Watch what you eat. I had already been coached on communication: speak slowly for the translator. Watch your use of humor—it doesn't always translate. Know the people's history. No matter how eager we were to get to India, certain arrangements and preparations were required. We had to get ready, or the trip could have proven chaotic, stressful, and unproductive.

When the angel showed up in Peter's cell, he brought with him not just a Word—"Get up quickly"—but a series of critical directives. Peter was about to go somewhere. He, too, needed to get ready. To this point, Peter's prison break had been a pretty abrupt experience: the angel showed up. A light came on. The angel hit Peter and said,

"Get up quickly." Peter's chains fell off. So far, not a lot of wasted inter-action. Of course, there wasn't much time for a flowery exchange—the prison was about to become the starting point for Peter's death walk—and the rest of his encounter with the angel proceeded in a similarly concise fashion. Right after the chains fell off, the angel gave a few brief, staccato instructions. We read: "'Put on your clothes and sandals.' And Peter did so. 'Wrap your cloak around you and follow me'" (Acts 12:8, TNIV).

"Put on your clothes and sandals"—or "Get dressed"—would seem a natural follow-up to "Get up quickly." Peter is about to go outside. The angel has already been there and knows the conditions. He is saying, "Get ready. Get prepared. We're moving out, and you've got to be able to survive where I'm taking you." Still, I must admit, if I were in Peter's position, I would probably be just lazy enough to have this thought: *Hold up. You've walked through walls. There's a light on in here. My chains fell off. The guards are dazed. Shouldn't you be able to do something to make my clothes jump on my body? I ought to be able to look down and see my shoes clap right onto my feet. We've got all these miracles going on in here—why do I have to stop and pull this tunic over my head and lace up these sandals with all of these strings? We're wasting time, aren't we?*

I might appear a bit conflicted when I say that the answer to my hypothetical question is, "No, we're not wasting time at all." What we're seeing here is more of that "take responsibility" principle. The first thing Peter had to do when the angel showed up and started talking was to decide to get up. That was responsibility number one: to decide to try. Peter did, and God made getting up possible, knocking off Peter's chains. Now, seconds later, we're seeing an extension of the same principle. Peter is standing in front of the angel, and what should happen but that he finds himself facing an onrush of new responsibilities. Is it unfair? No, it isn't.

Here's the thing about God: qhen He gets ready to move you out of your limitations, you can count on Him—He will do what only He can do. A light will come on. Guards will stay oblivious. Chains will fall off. These are things only God can do. But putting on your shoes? You can handle that. Getting into your clothes and throwing on a coat? You can do those things. You don't need a miracle to do them. Those are aspects of getting ready that you can take care of yourself.

Often, when God performs miracles in our lives—miracles of answered prayer for our children, reconciliation in our relationships, change in our hearts, deliverance from emotional issues, provision for our needs—we thank Him for what He has done, but then we keep sitting around, asking Him to do more. I can imagine His response: "Listen, I'll keep doing My part, but I need you to make sure you handle your part. I'll lead you out of the prison and take you into the city. I'll change your heart. I'll change the hearts of others toward you. I'll do the things you can't possibly do. But you must make the adjustments you can make. That's your responsibility."

As we track with Peter on his way out of prison, we will see this principle operating along the way: when something needs to be handled supernaturally, God will do it; but when something arises that Peter can do, God will require him to do it. At this juncture—as Peter stands unchained amid the dazed guards—God is asking him to get ready to move. Just as I had to prepare myself to travel to India, Peter must prepare himself to embark on another leg of his Next Level journey...and so must you. Remember, God has been preparing you all along in your prison. Since you first landed in your limitations, God has been doing miraculous internal work in your heart. Now, He's simply asking you to do a few things so you can break out of your limitations in confidence, having your act together, being prepared. Our release into the next phase of our journey—and our ability to thrive in that next phase—is contingent on our obedience.

A LIFESTYLE OF OBEDIENCE

Just as limitations and prison experiences teach us obedience, so do prison breaks. In something as risky as breaking away from those guards, we don't want to be the ones leading ourselves. We've been locked up. We don't know where we're going. We have no idea how to pull off an escape or where to go to avoid discovery. God must lead the way; and if He is going to lead us, then we must be able to follow— to obey, sometimes blindly, so we don't end up busted and imprisoned yet again. Once we get to the city and begin the next phase of the journey, then, too, obedience is what preserves us. We've never been this way before. Following God is imperative if we want to stay on the path and keep walking in His plans.

Obedience must become our first response—an almost instinctual response—when God speaks. Even when we struggle in our attempts to follow His instructions—even when our thinking is clouded with ulterior motives—ultimately, obedience must remain our primary intention and become our lifestyle. Obedience doesn't have to be intimidating; it springs right out of our friendship with God. When we love Him, as any lover can attest, we want to please Him. When we fall in love with God, we want to do what He says as a matter of course. Obedience is a love thing. Jesus said, "He who has My commandments and keeps them is the one who loves Me" (John 14:21, NASB). He also said, "If anyone loves Me, he will keep My word" (John 14:23, NASB), and, "You are My friends if you do what I command you" (John 15:14, NASB). The lover of God obeys God. Jesus states it as a fact.

Further, because we love God and realize that He loves us, not only do we want to make Him happy by doing what He says, but we also trust that He has good reasons for the commands He gives. Now, our faith in God is operating. We trust that our Friend wants the best for us. We trust that His motives toward us are pure. Peter is about to leave the prison. It's pretty obvious that he would benefit by wearing clothes and shoes. God is not giving a frivolous command. God is efficient. He doesn't waste anything. If He tells us we need something, then we need it. In faith, we must lock on to that truth.

A call to get ready is a signpost on the journey; it says we are about to move into new territory. When God gives us a command, He is signaling expansion. From this angle, God's "Get ready" commands should fuel us in our third Next Level heart attitude—a heart of expectancy toward God—and in our desire to obey Him. If I know God's commands come to indicate growth, prepare me for the future, and work for my good—and I know this because the commands are coming from my Friend—then I become energized to put my faith into action and obey Him. Each time I do, my faith grows stronger, my friendship with God deepens, and I become motivated to continue in a lifestyle of obedience.

PUT ON YOUR CLOTHES

Let's break down what the angel instructed Peter to do. "Put on your clothes." Clothing is particularly helpful when we are (a) stepping out of doors into the elements and (b) stepping out of an isolated prison into the public street. You don't want God to speak to you like your parents may have: "Son, I know you're not going outside dressed like that," or, "Yeah, that's a nice outfit...but where's the rest of it?" When God begins to break you out of limitations and expand your life, you must be properly clothed.

I'm not talking about natural clothes. I'm talking about wearing the proper spiritual clothes—living and carrying yourself in a way that honors God. You've been locked up, living in a limited place all the time God has been developing you. Now, pick up what God has created in your life and put it on. Pick up that new level of discipline, trust in God, commitment, inner strength, stamina, and maturity of character. Clothe yourself with those new habits that have deepened your friendship with God—your time spent in prayer, worship, and the Word. Build yourself up in your faith. In order to handle the influence God desires to give you on your journey and impact the lives of others for Him, you must recognize the call to represent God. You can't do all the things you used to do. You've got to be dressed right.

When God says, "It's time to leave the prison," your personal business is no longer your personal business. The old way of thinking was this: *What I do is my business. Where I go is my business. Who I spend time with—that's my business.* But everything pertaining to us has something to do with God. What we do matters. What we say matters. What we think and do in "private" matters, because those internal, private issues will work their way out into the open. Every decision you make reflects on the One you serve. If you are ready to come out of limitations, you must be willing to commit to certain adjustments. You've already adjusted your thinking—you've come to see your friendship with God as your life's primary purpose. Now you must take responsibility for how you, as a friend of God, "dress."

Once, when I was scheduled to preach a service in a state correctional facility, I decided I wanted to do so dressed just like the prisoners. I told the prison administration, "When I come, I want to look like the men who are there. I want to wear the same light blue denims and the dark shirt with the number on it. I want all of that. Shoes. Everything. I want to connect with them and be a part of who they are."

The response I got from the prison was swift and resounding. "Oh, no," they said. "You can't dress like everybody else. Not if you plan on leaving." Notice the operative word—leaving. They said, "If you plan on coming and leaving, then you've got to wear your street clothes. You don't have to wear a tie or a collar, but you do have to wear something different from the prisoners because, once visiting hours are up, the only folk who can leave the prison are those who are dressed differently."

When God calls you out of limitations, you can't be dressed like everybody else—unless you want to stay locked up. If you want out, you've got to live and act differently than those who have no desire to obey God. Don't be afraid. God is with you to help you. He knows you're not perfect. When you start to fear you're going to blow it—when you fear you won't be able to identify things like integrity and character, let alone put them on—keep returning to the process of obedience. It starts with your decision: "Lord, I want to get up quickly. I want to put on the right clothes. I want my heart and my life to look the way You need them to look. But I need Your help. I'm too weak to do this. I don't even trust my own heart. All I can do is decide to obey You and decide to believe You will help me. I believe. Help my unbelief!"

PUT ON YOUR SHOES

"Put on your sandals, Peter."

We often talk about responsibility as if it is something to be dreaded—a burden, a weight, a negative. But think about where we are: God is breaking us out of prison! We need to get excited about these new responsibilities. So what if we have to put on our own shoes? Shoes mean we're going somewhere.

Growing up, I didn't often walk around the house or the yard wearing shoes. Much of the time, I just wore shoes when I went out. Shoes meant travel, change, activity. Even today, that principle applies to me. I don't wear shoes at home—we have white carpet, and with five kids, even if some of them are grown, the rules about shoes are taken seriously. Shoes come off in the house; they go back on when you leave. If you see me putting on my shoes, that means I'm going out—it's time for a change of environment.

Shoes also determine the activities in which we're about to engage. You don't play basketball in high heels. You don't play tennis in hiking boots—not if you're trying to play well. And you don't ride a motor-cycle in flip-flops if you want to keep your feet. When God gets ready to break us out of prison, not only will He instruct us to put on our shoes, but He also may specify which shoes—that is, He may prompt us to prepare ourselves for specific activities.

Maybe we need to enroll in classes and add to our vocational qual-ifications. Maybe we need to cultivate new, strategic relationships. Maybe we need to discipline ourselves to write up the business plan that's been rolling around in our heads for the last two years. Maybe we need to begin reading deeply about a certain subject. Barefoot works in a tight, limited place; it works when you don't have any-where to go. But when God says, "It's time to move," we must ready ourselves for the change. In Peter's case, that meant putting on his sandals—his walking shoes.

TESTIMONY SHOES

Our shoes not only speak of where we're going; they also speak of where we've been. Let's say this is a detective show and you're a sus-pect for a crime carried out in Central Park. You deny involvement, claiming, "I haven't been to Central Park in fourteen years. I don't ride the train anywhere near Central Park. I don't take cabs in that area or even get on a bus going by."

The officer looks you in the eye and asks, "Are you sure? We've confiscated a pair of your shoes and identified a certain kind of dirt on the soles that can only be found in Central Park. It can't be found in Jersey, Brooklyn, or Queens. The only place you can find this dirt is

Central Park. Besides that, it's fresh dirt. We know you've been there, and it hasn't been that long ago."

When God brings you out of limitations, the soles of your shoes will still be carrying a little dirt—evidence of the places you've walked is coming out of the prison with you. You haven't been perfect all your life. You haven't had it straight forever. You were just in Central Park two days ago—it's okay to admit it. The dirt on your shoes tells the story. Just like the rest of us, you've been places you would rather not remember.

But I have good news: Your dirt is a testimony. It's not there to condemn you. That dirt means you've walked through some tough experiences and that God has delivered you! Don't ever be ashamed of the broken places you've left. Your journey is a testimony of God's faithfulness. Don't try to hide those shoes—put them on! And when you put them on, remember the second Next Level heart attitude, a heart of gratitude to God. Learn to say, "God, I thank You. I haven't always been right, but You've been with me every step of the way. I haven't always done it like I should have. There's evidence on my shoes. But You brought me out of those places. You showed up and brought me out, and I'm not the same. This dirt is just here to remind me. Thank You, God, for the testimony of my shoes!"

When the angel appears with a light and a list of commands, obey the Word of God. Strap on those sandals. Peter had to put on the same old shoes he'd been wearing all along. Put on your shoes and rejoice over the story of God's rescue in your life. That story will become important as you continue on your journey, enter the city, and begin to influence others. You need your testimony. You need that dirt. You need evidence. Otherwise, the hurting people God sends your way won't get the kind of encouragement they need. They need to know what God has done for you.

Take some time to remember where you've been and to appreciate what the dirt signifies: the faithfulness of God. Go out with praise—this is your moment! You're breaking out of limitations. This is what you've longed to do. Say, "God, I'm coming out! Thank You that I'm not where I used to be. Thank You for staying with me. Thank You that it's time for new places and a new season of friendship with You!"

CONTINUE TO FOLLOW

Notice what the Acts 12 passage says about Peter once the angel finished telling him what to put on: it says, simply, "And he did so." Then the angel said, "Wrap your cloak around you and follow me." And guess what Peter did? He obeyed. We read, "And he went out and continued to follow" (Acts 12:8-9, ESV). Continued to follow. This is how we journey with God at the Next Level. We don't obey just once or twice. Getting ready—all that we do to break out of prison—is a process, even as growing while we're in our limitations is a process. We have to keep our faith awake, release our frustration, and work on those first three Next Level heart attitudes—pressing into our friendship with God, maintaining a heart of gratitude, and building ourselves up in expectation. Getting dressed takes time. We don't get dressed in a few minutes. We follow God in faith as He leads us through a series of preparations.

Preparation is not just for our benefit. I prepared for the trip to India not just because I wanted things to go smoothly for me, but also because I knew that God planned to use the gifts He had been building into my life for the good of other people. I needed to be ready for the sake of the people to whom I would minister. For Peter, too, readiness was required so he could go back to the people he led—the church—and minister effectively to them. The believers in Jerusalem had been scrambling since his arrest, holding prayer meetings day and night. They desperately needed Peter, and God had chosen him. God's plans for Peter's journey, for his path of life, were part of a vision much greater than Peter himself.

You may not see yourself as a leader in the way Peter was a leader, but you have something that other people need. God created you with gifts. You carry something in your heart—a dream, a desire, a vision—that, when it influences the hearts of others, can be a great blessing. As you break out of your limitations and begin another phase of your Next Level journey, your lifestyle of obedience will become critical in new ways. Now, other people are involved. Now, you are connecting with plans that touch more than just your own life. This is what all of the preparation, the getting dressed, was for—for your entrance into the city, the community, the place where people need light. Like the helium balloons rising into the India night are the lives of those whom God will use you to touch—lives made free, lives like dreams, like prayers, flying high.

Mapping Your Next Level Leadership Journey

MILE MARKER: WHERE AM I ON THE JOURNEY?

As you arise to lead in the next phase of your journey and you start to "get dressed," have you thought of anything you need to wear? New habits, disciplines, relationships, possibly? Or maybe you need to clean up some old relationships and move forward?

_____

_____

_____

_____

Peter had to lace up his shoes. As you enter the next half of the game, where do you need to tighten up your walk?

_____

_____

_____

_____

CHARTING YOUR COURSE: FOCUSING ON THE PATH AHEAD

I have discovered that I often know what to do, but I need help remaining consistent. At times, it was my wife; at other times, my ministry colleagues; but at other seasons, I needed to hire a coach—someone whose primary focus was keeping me on track. What definitive steps should you prepare to take in this season of your leadership growth?

LEADER'S PRAYER: ASKING FOR GUIDANCE

"Lord don't allow me to do the same things while expecting different results! Speak to my heart and mind the new thing that You are doing inside me, and show me who to ask for help and accountability as I take the next steps. In Jesus' name, amen."

LEADER'S WORD: RECEIVING
GUIDANCE FROM HIS WORD

"For I am about to do something new. See, I have already begun! Do you not see it? I will make a pathway through the wilderness. I will create rivers in the dry wasteland." —Isaiah 43:19 (NLT)

PART 4

MOVING FORWARD AT THE NEXT LEVEL

CHAPTER 9

———

———

—————

WALKING OUT

"I am hurrying," I whisper, fumbling with my sandals as the man wrapped in light urges me again. Quickly.

I look at the two guards standing against the wall. Chains lead from their wrists to where I was just sitting between them, yet they seem completely unaware. Is this real? Am I dreaming? The man in light steps out of the cell and into the passage.

"Follow me," he says.

I grab my cloak, throw it around myself hastily, and move with him, just able to make out his form in the pillar of light. As we go, I shake my arms to wake myself, expecting to feel the familiar weight of the chains—and beneath me, the hard stone seat—but I feel nothing. The Light-Man walks on quickly.

Winding our way through the maze of passages, I become aware of something in my heart: uneasiness. Caution? No. It is fear. Fear. I am thinking ahead to our exit—to the guards keeping watch at the door and, after them, the guards at their posts along the way. Will they see us? What will they do?

Keeping close to the Light-Man, I think back to another night walk—this one in Galilee. The storm on the sea, the blackness of night, the wind battering our boat as if it were a toy—we were all there but Jesus. He had sent us ahead in the boat and gone to the mountain to pray.

Then, suddenly, late in the night, a figure appeared on the sea, walking toward us in the squall. We could barely make it out. A light? A formation of clouds? No: a man, unfazed, unwavering, as if He were walking on land. "A ghost! An apparition!" we cried.

But then, a voice—the Master's: "Don't be scared! I'm here! It's Me!"

Could it be? Was this really the Master? Could we trust this figure, a blur in the tumult of the storm? Someone had to speak up, and usually, I was that someone.

"Jesus!" I called. "If it's really You, then ask me to walk out on the water with You!"

That was my test for Him. Jesus was my friend; we were close. In tight situations, Jesus usually chose only John, James, and me to accompany Him. I knew how the Master walked. I had seen Him perform many miracles—even restore to life people who had died. I knew His way, His manner. I knew Him. Surely, the way to be certain this Man was my friend was to have Him call me to walk with Him out in the storm. So I yelled out over the water, "If it's You, then let me walk with You!"

"Come on!" He yelled back.

Yes—now that was the Master. It was Jesus. I climbed out of the boat into the water and, instantly, found myself walking—walking to Jesus in the turbulent blackness, walking to the only steady Thing in the chaos and noise of the squall. Then, without warning, the storm intensified. Water surged over me. Wind overpowered my senses. There was the figure, the Man, reaching toward me, but fear—fear washed over me like a thousand waves, and I froze. I began to sink.

"Rescue me!" I yelled. A burning in my chest. My body submerged, scrambling. Where was the surface? Then...His hand. His voice. Perfect stability. Air.

I had thought Jesus walking on the water was the real miracle. Then, I thought walking on water myself was the miracle—for who was I? I was not Jesus. But thrown about violently by the waves, preparing to go under and never come up, I experienced the greatest miracle of all. For it was Jesus lifting me—walking on that water with me in His grip—that changed me. There in the dark, I saw the fierce love of my Friend. Even if He had to carry me, Jesus would do what it took to keep us walking together.

Now, arriving with the Light-Man at the door of the prison—*Is it real?*—I wonder. *Could this walk out into the night, into territory patrolled by guards who know who I am, who serve at the pleasure of Herod, who plan to come for me at daybreak—could this treacherous walk be as another night walk with Jesus? For if it is, then I can do it. I will do it. Yes! Even if it is a dream, Jesus, let's take another walk!*

THIS IS REAL

The Bible says that, as Peter followed the angel, "he did not know that what was being done by the angel was real, but thought he was seeing a vision" (Acts 12:9, NASB). As we will see, Peter is in for a literal awakening. He may not know it yet, but he will: this is no dream. Peter is walking through those passageways, approaching a prison door flanked by armed guards, and he is about to walk out into the night. This exit on the heels of an angel of the Lord—this walk out of limitations—this is real.

As Peter follows the angel out, he is going to need everything God built into him during his prison time—and so are you. Walking out takes courage. It takes faith. Here is Peter, a man who walked into the prison under heavy security, now being challenged to walk out on his own, as if the threat posed by those guards was immaterial. That's a scary proposition. Those guards are just as dangerous as they were before. Granted, Peter has just seen the guards in his cell remain oblivious to the angel, but there's no guarantee the same will be true of the other guards Peter must pass.

You may be in Peter's shoes right now: you've experienced being thrown into prison. You've gotten closer to God in prison. You've developed stamina and character in prison. In all, you've experienced growth you never thought possible. But now, it's time to walk out of the prison; and walking out, though exhilarating, will entail facing some obstacles you faced unsuccessfully in the past. This is showtime. In a few moments, you've got to put this book down, walk out of your limitations, and confront what might not have worked for you before. As I said, it's a scary proposition—or, at least, a disturbing one.

Can I give you some great news? You are empowered by God for this moment! You have all that you need. Everything required of you can be found in your friendship with God. Consider Peter: in moments of crisis and trepidation, he could draw on his friendship with Jesus. Here was a man so passionate about Jesus that he jumped out of a boat during a storm to get to Him (Matthew 14:22-33). Finding his footing on the sea, Peter might have thought, *Jesus, all I really understand is what I'm doing right now—walking with You. I don't understand the theology—how You're the Son of God, how You plan to save the lost—but I've been walking with You these two or three years, and I do understand that.*

You can say the same thing as you walk out of your prison. In the past, you may not have understood who you really are. You may have seen yourself the way those Israelite spies saw themselves—as grasshoppers. But as you've grown more intimate with God, you've begun to see things differently. You understand who you are—God's empowered friend. You understand where you are—at the Next Level. Walking out of limitations may take courage; but, like Peter, you've been walking with God all along, and you know firsthand what God can do. Your faith is awake and operating. You aren't mustering some flimsy, phony courage that says, "Okay, I'm going to try to be brave here." The courage you have is authentic. You know God. You've learned to trust Him. And whether He needs you to jump out of a boat or walk past some guards in the middle of the night, you can do it. This is the path of life. God is walking with you and, if need be, He will carry you in His arms.

STICKING WITH THE ANGEL

Peter may have walked out of prison in a daze, but he knew to do one thing—stick close to the angel. When you walk out of limitations, you may feel a little groggy and off your game at first, but you must continue to follow God's lead. Don't lose the angel! When you're Herod's prized prisoner-on-the-run and guards are patrolling the area, you don't want to take the wrong road.

But what if I can't see where God is leading me? How can I walk out if I don't know where to go? These are legitimate questions. So often, the path of life is difficult to discern. We can't always see the way. We can't make out God's direction. We vacillate. We lose confidence. It's dark out there! In these moments, as Peter must have done, we draw on our friendship with God and make a decision to trust Him. In Proverbs, we read, "Trust in the Lord with all your heart and do not lean on your own understanding. In all your ways acknowledge Him, and He will make your paths straight" (Proverbs 3:5-6, NASB).

Trusting God wholeheartedly speaks of total dependence on Him. That is what it means to stick with the angel. We thought we were desperate for God in the confines and restrictions of our prison. We thought we were desperate for Him when circumstances seemed to line up against us, when loved ones left us, or when we fell into destructive habits. But in times of release from limitations, we come up against our need for God in a new way. We're so accustomed to limited spaces that we don't know what to do when we become mobile. Now, we realize our potential to make wrong turns, to become exhausted, to lose pace; the loneliness and intensity we've just endured in prison can catch up with us and cause us to hurt. On our

journey out of limitations, we need to seek God—a heart to seek God
is our fourth Next Level heart attitude.

Next Level Heart Attitudes
1. A Heart for Friendship with God
2. A Heart of Gratitude to God
3. A Heart of Expectancy Toward God
4. A HEART TO SEEK GOD

Jesus said, "Ask, and it will be given to you; seek, and you will find;
knock, and it will be opened to you" (Matthew 7:7, NASB). Jesus'
emphasis here is persistence. The original Greek verbs used for ask,
seek, and knock imply continual action. "Ask, and keep asking," Jesus
was saying. "Seek, and keep seeking. Knock, and keep knocking." In
other words, like so much else on our friendship journey, seeking
God is a process. We may not get the answers as quickly as we would
like; but if we keep seeking, eventually, we will find.

Seeking God requires faith. Remember what we read in Hebrews:
"He who comes to God must believe that He is and that He is a
rewarder of those who seek Him" (Hebrews 11:6, NASB). If we go to
God for guidance, we must believe that He is going to give it. We must
expect our Friend to give it. Do you see how all of our Next Level
heart attitudes work together? As friends of God, when we seek Him,

we expect Him to reward us. We then thank Him in advance, because we know our Friend wants us to make it. Do you believe God wants you to know His will? This isn't hide-and-seek. God isn't hiding His will while you stand in the middle of the yard, counting with your eyes closed. God is on your side. He wants you to take the right road. He wants you to stay on the path.

As you seek God, begin to practice some of the faith principles that have brought you to this point. Base your hope on God's Word and meditate on His truth. You can start with the verses quoted in this section of the chapter. Memorize these verses. Repeat them regularly to yourself. Declare them over your situation and pray them back to God. Say, "Lord, I make the decision to trust You with all of my heart, and I believe that, as I walk out of these limitations, You will make my paths straight." And, "Lord, Your Word promises that, as I seek and keep seeking, I will find. That means I can trust You to meet me when I seek You. Even when I can't see where to go, I choose to expect Your direction and help."

As you engage with the Word of God this way, allow God's truth to replace any words of doubt, indecision, or fear that may hold sway in your heart or mind. Speak the Word, not as an incantatory formula to make God answer you; rather, now that the Word has become more real to you, speak out of a renewed mind and a heart that believes. Paul wrote, "We ... believe, therefore we also speak" (2 Corinthians 4:13, NASB).

Continually dialoguing with God and placing your trust in Him builds your friendship with Him. Loving God is the way you wait on God. Waiting for His direction doesn't have to produce frustration.

Yes, you want direction; but you are not waiting just for that. We've considered the kind of waiting described here in Isaiah: "Yet those who wait for the Lord will gain new strength" (Isaiah 40:31, NASB). Remember, in this verse, the word used for "wait" speaks of waiting in an engaged, excited manner—much as a waiter or server in a restaurant would do. As you wait for God's guidance on your way out of prison, you do so serving Him, doing whatever He asks, and anticipating His desires. This is faith-waiting—and it will be fulfilled.

Ultimately, seeking God is not what we do just when we need answers or direction. We seek God first for Himself—to get close to Him. We seek the One we love. In the Song of Solomon, the beloved, desperate for her lover, roams the city searching for him. Once she finds him, she gets as close to him as she can. She says, "I held on to him and would not let him go until I had brought him to my mother's house, and into the room of her who conceived me" (Song of Solomon 3:4, NASB). Before anything else, we seek God because we long for him and desperately desire intimacy with our Friend. Once in His presence, we find everything else that we need (Psalm 16:11; 36:9).

WALKING PAST THE GUARDS

God's guidance comes to us in many ways. Primarily, He directs us through His Word, but also through circumstances, people, our own hearts, and other means. Sometimes, we don't even recognize God's leading—we just find ourselves in the right place. After Peter started following the angel, the next thing we learn is that he has walked past the first and second guards who, likely, were posted at gates in the city walls. One minute, Peter is walking out of his cell; the next minute, he is walking through gates.

Historians describe ancient Jerusalem as having been ringed by three walls, each with a gate. The prison where Peter was held may have been built into the outermost wall, and the first and second guards posted on the gates to the outer and middle walls of the city. A squad of soldiers—four guards—may have been posted at each gate, meaning that, when Peter went by the first and second guards, he actually may have gone by two groups of four guards, one squad per gate.

Not only did Peter pass these guards without incident, but some translations of the Bible also seem to "pencil" the guards into the narrative as if they're a side note. The guards don't even show up in the main part of the sentence; they're thrown into an introductory clause, almost as if the idea of a fugitive walking by several armed soldiers is nothing out of the ordinary. It reads, "When they [the angel and Peter] had passed the first and second guard ...." (Acts 12:10, NASB). When they had passed—as if it were a given! That tells you something about the way God saw those guards. They were just part of the landscape—important in that they belonged in Peter's testimony but unable to interfere with God's plan to move Peter on, as we see confirmed in the main clause of the sentence: "They [the angel and Peter] came to the iron gate that leads into the city"—that is, to the final gate (Acts 12:10, NASB).

As you move forward at the Next Level, you may find yourself struggling with issues that have haunted you in the past. These are your first and second guards. In order to get to the city's innermost gate and go in, you're going to have to walk past these guards again.

Whether your guards are bad decisions, relationship challenges, personal setbacks you were unable to overcome, or other issues, you must walk by them to reach the city and begin the next phase of your journey. In the process, you may find yourself battling discouraging memories and emotions. You may feel overwhelmed by fear. You may wonder, *What's going to be different when I go by the guards this time?* The difference this time is that now it is God's time for your release.

This is the time in life when you must try some things again. Recognize where you are on your journey, and take full advantage of your "Now" season. The Bible teaches us to "walk circumspectly … redeeming the time, because the days are evil" (Ephesians 5:15-16, NKJV). As you walk out of limitations, look around you; make the most of your opportunities. You are no longer living in prison. You can take initiative. You can travel from one place to another. Ask God to help you understand His plans. Continue in our fourth Next Level heart attitude, a heart to seek God. The passage in Ephesians says, "Therefore do not be unwise, but understand what the will of the Lord is" (Ephesians 5:17, NKJV). If the Bible tells us to understand the Lord's will, then we can understand it.

Maybe you thought God would never give you a chance to try certain things again. Maybe you turned your back on God the last time you walked by the guards, and you don't believe you deserve another chance. Maybe you became discouraged, lacked support from others, or faced so much adversity when you tried before that you accepted defeat as the norm. Whatever the case, the only way those guards can keep you from walking into God's plans now is if you allow them to keep you from trying. Don't be intimidated. God may let those guards remain at their posts, but He has neutralized their ability to act. Try again! You have the faith. Exercise that third Next Level heart attitude, a heart of expectancy toward God.

You may feel anxious as you begin to walk, but as you put one foot in front of the other, you notice something unusual: the guards keeping watch at the first gate don't even seem to see you go by. You take a second look. Yes—you saw it right the first time. Those guards are standing at their posts, not even glancing in your direction. You press on, through the second gate at the middle wall, and those guards, too, seem oblivious. You feel stunned, but this is real. You begin to thank God. He has just done something you could never do yourself—shut the guards down. Then, suddenly, you put the guards out of your mind. Something ahead has captured your attention. It is the iron gate—the gate leading into the city—and beyond it, in darkness, Jerusalem, fanned out over the hills.

COMING TO THE GATE

Through the bars of the gate, you can barely make out the form of Jerusalem's cityscape, shadowy in the predawn hours. Jerusalem: "City of Peace." You've imagined the city, dreamed of it in prison. You've envisioned its streets, the look of this or that prospect, the markets, the bustle, the life. You fell in love with God in prison; you found contentment in Him and new strength. But you longed for the city—longed to be free and a part of its flow.

Now, as you stand facing the gate, you feel exhilarated but nervous. Your focus shifts. You examine the bars and wonder, *How do I get through? How do I go in?* To this point, the path you've followed out of prison has been clear, unobstructed. You walked by the guards with ease and passed through the first two gates. Now, here you are at the final, innermost gate—stopped. Again, you take in the view of the sleeping city. You're here—right at the threshold. But will this gate actually open? Have you come this far only to be disappointed?

Why would God break you out of prison just to stop you at a barrier He doesn't intend to help you overcome? Why would He teach you how to walk with Him in friendship, how to enjoy Him in limitations, how to trust Him, and follow Him out, only to have you hit a wall you will never get past? He has brought you this far—freed you, given you victory over the guards that used to hold you, swung open those first two gates of impossibility. Now, one final gate stands between you and the city. Don't shut down your dream. Don't let frustration creep in. Keep looking through the bars of that gate. Look with all of the expectation and joy that overwhelmed you as you first caught sight of the view. Draw on your Next Level heart attitudes: Expect God to act. Thank Him in advance. Rest in the arms of your Friend. You've done your part—followed Him and walked out. Now God will be faithful to do His.

MIRACLE AT THE GATE

What happened next for Peter only merits a few words in the Acts account—another reminder that, for God, miracles are not a strain. The complete sentence reads: "When they had passed the first and second guard, they came to the iron gate that leads into the city, which opened for them *by itself*" (Acts 12:10, NASB, emphasis added).

Picture this for a moment. Peter and the angel make it to the gate that leads into the city. Once they get there, suddenly, the gate opens for them—by itself. At this point, Peter still thought he was dreaming, which makes sense. Imagine it: you're looking at a massive, iron gate, wondering how you're going to get through, when you begin to hear a deep groaning sound—so deep you can feel it in your chest. Slowly, the gate begins to open and, in seconds, you have enough space to pass through and enter the city. One minute, you're blocked; the next minute, you have passage. This is no gimmick, and no one else is around. Standing with the angel, you realize the magnitude of what has just happened—God Himself has opened the gate.

The picture of the gate opening for Peter represents at least two things God may be doing in your life right now. First, here at the threshold of the city, God is opening gates in your thinking. The Bible says of a person, "For as he thinks in his heart, so is he" (Proverbs 23:7, NKJV). After walking this far on your road out of limitations, one thing that could keep you from entering the city is flawed thinking. If the head is still in prison, then the body can't very well walk through that gate.

Peter was the leader of the church in Jerusalem. Naturally, his arrest and imprisonment impacted the church community. Because their leader, or "head," was sitting in a prison cell awaiting trial—and likely execution—the "body" was living in emergency mode. People were praying day and night, and the life of the community was disrupted. Similarly, when a person's head is imprisoned—when thinking is limited or flawed—the whole life will be affected. God wants to open up gates of new insight and understanding about His ways and plans so that our lives, too, will open up in new ways.

Ask God to show you the areas in your thinking that He wants to change. Are you struggling to believe some truth in His Word? Do you see principles you don't understand operating in your life? Do you believe you are missing out on some aspect of intimacy with God and want to know Him better? Apply our fourth Next Level heart attitude, a heart to seek God, and ask Him for the wisdom you need. Spend time in God's Word. Recognize your inability to change your own mind, and invite God to open up gates in your thinking. He will respond. The Bible promises, "But if any of you lacks wisdom, let him ask of God, who gives to all generously and without reproach, and it will be given to him" (James 1:5, NASB).

Changes in our thinking impact not only our lives but also the lives of others. Peter was about to experience a thinking change—he was about to enter the city, wake up from his daze, and recognize that his release was real—and his altered perspective had the power to transform the church. The people would see that God had moved in response to their prayers. Their faith in God's ability to work miracles would increase. Having suffered under Herod's persecutions, they would now be strengthened and reenergized to do the will of God in the city.

God wants to change your thinking and help you better understand His ways and plans so that you can more effectively influence the lives of those who respect and follow you. A city speaks of people. By bringing you out of the isolation of prison and up to the city gate, God is signaling His plan to release influence through your life into the lives of others. Jesus said the second greatest commandment is to love our neighbor as ourselves (Mark 12:31). When Peter stood at the Jerusalem gate, he was standing at the gate of the city he was called to serve. The city is the place of your freedom, but it is also the place of your service.

Just as God opens gates in our thinking when we get to the city, so He opens certain gates in our life circumstances. We've tried very hard to push these gates open ourselves. We've tried to make relationships work and opportunities happen. We've tried to make things in our lives move. But no matter how determined we became in our efforts, we couldn't produce the changes we desired. Can you think of a few such gates that wouldn't budge no matter how hard you pushed? The psalmist wrote, "Unless the Lord builds the house, they labor in vain who build it" (Psalm 127:1, NASB). We could say the same of certain gates in our lives: either God must open them, or we can forget it.

I don't know how Peter felt watching the Jerusalem gate swing open by itself, but I do know how I feel when I watch God work circumstances out for me that I never could've engineered. For example, several months after my wife and I moved our family to Norfolk, I put together enough funding to buy television time for the ministry in our market. All we could afford was an eleven o'clock spot on Sunday nights; but almost immediately, I started believing God wanted us to reach more people than our late-night spot would allow.

Being a bold, 31-year-old pastor—one with absolutely no name recognition—I told our account executive at the station that we wanted the prime spot for ministry programming: eight o'clock on Sunday mornings. The executive didn't tell me until much later, but he apparently found my declaration laughable (1) because the cost of the spot was so high and (2) because a well-known ministry currently held the spot. The chance of the station letting us have it was basically nil. Still, I knew that, in order to reach more people, we needed a better spot. For some strange reason, I started to believe this prime spot for ministry eventually would be ours.

Several months later, I got a call from the account executive. I remember the conversation this way: getting right down to business, he said, "You know that Sunday morning spot you've been wanting? Well, we just got a call from the ministry that has it, and they're coming off the air."

"Really?" I asked. I could feel my body tense up. I was thinking, *Is he offering the spot to me? And if he is, can we find the money to do it?*

"Let me explain," he went on. "The ministry is coming off the air now—as in this week. Not only do I need you to consider taking the spot permanently, but I also need to ask if you will allow us to run your program for free in that spot until you decide."

I might as well have been Peter standing at the Jerusalem gate as it opened. Was I dreaming? Was I seeing a vision? They were offering, and temporarily giving, me the spot? In a word, yes—they were. God threw open that gate. We jumped on the opportunity and have held the spot ever since.

NOW, GO THROUGH IT

At this stage on your Next Level journey, some of the gates God swings open for you may have a dreamlike quality to them, but they are opening. Just as you had to walk past your guards, now you must walk through the open gates. After the Jerusalem gate opened for Peter and the angel, one translation reads, "They went through it" (Acts 12:10, TNIV). Now that you've been freed from prison and led back to the city—now that you've seen the intimidating city gate open by itself—what do you do? You do the obvious thing: you go through it.

When God brings us out of one thing, He does so in order to bring us into something new. God didn't bring Peter out of prison to leave him standing at the gate to the city. God's intention was to bring Peter out in order to bring him in. When Moses urged the Israelites to obey God and encouraged them about the good things God was reserving for them in the Promised Land, he told the people to be ready to recount to their children the miraculous way God had brought them out of slavery in Egypt—"with a mighty hand." But Moses didn't stop there. He moved on in the narrative, saying of God, "He brought us out from there in order to bring us in, to give us the land which He had sworn to our fathers" (Deuteronomy 6:21-23, NASB).

God brought the people out of Egypt in a great spectacle, but their release was only the prelude to something else: their entrance into the land. The same is true for you. God has broken you out of your limitations, and that is something to celebrate. Celebrating our release experiences is a critical part of our friendship with God, an expression of our second Next Level heart attitude, a heart of gratitude to God. But don't miss what God is doing now. He brought you out of prison so that He could bring you into the city. Celebrate the past, but do so in order to embrace your future. God knows the plans that He has for you—"to give you a future and a hope" (Jeremiah 29:11, NASB). He fulfilled certain parts of His plans during your prison phase; but now, it is time for you to operate in the plans He ordained for your city phase. The gate is standing open, and you get to decide. Will you embrace this new season? Will you exercise your faith and go through?

Mapping Your Next Level Leadership Journey

MILE MARKER: WHERE AM I ON THE JOURNEY?

In order to arrive at the next level of his leadership journey, Peter had to walk past several guards and through an iron gate—none of which he could do alone. What are the barriers that you must walk through?

_____

_____

_____

_____

Where will your faith and diligence need to be applied in order to get into the "city of your greater influence"?

_____

_____

_____

_____

Spend some time today and tomorrow describing the specific victories you're trusting God for as you lead more effectively.

CHARTING YOUR COURSE: FOCUSING ON THE PATH AHEAD

Draw from the strength of your friendship with God, not your knowledge about leadership principles. Those principles are great, but Peter had to know God before he could be an effective leader. As you remember your best friend status, determine to walk past the barriers. Pray for courage. Boldness. New faith. New vision.

LEADERS PRAYER: ASKING FOR GUIDANCE

"Lord, I'm trusting You and Your love for me at this stage of my leadership process. I now realize that it's not by my own power or might or knowledge that I've seen any success, but by friendship with Your Spirit. Help me courageously walk past every barrier and no longer be held captive to these limitations. In Jesus' name, amen."

LEADER'S WORD: RECEIVING GUIDANCE FROM HIS WORD

"Be strong and very courageous. Be careful to obey all the instructions Moses gave you. Do not deviate from them, turning either to the right or to the left. Then you will be successful in everything you do."
—*Joshua 1:7 (NLT)*

CHAPTER 10

COURAGE TO WALK ON

With the gate still in motion, the Light-Man presses through the gap and into the city. I try to stay close. We move swiftly along the road, and now, in the distance behind me, I can just hear the heavy gate swing closed.

The dark, narrow street is a blur of shapes—dark buildings and alley doors—but I know where we are. I know these streets—every turn, every climb. Through the soles of my sandals, I can feel the uneven road. I hear my steps padding steadily, then quickening. My eyes are on the Light-Man, who seems to glide, hovering over the street.

I watch for a sign, something the Lord might show me, some landmark the man might point out in my dream. *Speak, Lord,* my heart says now. *What is it You want me to see?*

We approach the first crossroads and stop. Which way? I glance left, then right, quickly; however, when I turn back, looking to see what the Light-Man will do, I see … nothing. Nothing! No one. No heavenly light. Only darkness—dark shapes, dark outlines, dark roads. The weight of my body sinks into my feet. The force of the road presses up through my sandals. A ghostly silence hangs over the street.

For the first time, I can feel myself breathe. My chest rises and falls. I inhale a draft of night air and slowly let it go. Alone. I am alone. Am I … ? No. Not dreaming. I'm here in the street, in the city. Conscious, awake, standing here on the road. This is real, not a vision. I'm free—rescued! God has done it. Yes! God Himself stopped the plans of my enemies and took me out of their hands. God sent His angel to lead me. God carried me out. God opened the gate. Now I know—it is God!

In the silence, I wait. Which way? Soon, darkness will lift. I consider my route and move out. Faster. Picking up pace. Now I can hear the voice of the tempter: "Yes, Peter, God brought you out. But look at you here, alone in the street. Where is God now? His angel has left you to fend for yourself just as Herod is waking up to the news that you're gone. Is that love? Look at you—exposed, set up for much worse. If you listen, you may even hear the sound of their horses …."

No. No! I move on, taking another turn, anticipating the bend in the street, moving. No—not alone. God is with me. I'm rescued, free, and I know where to go.

COURAGE TO CONTINUE

Once Peter wakes up and realizes he isn't dreaming, continuing on becomes a life-threatening enterprise. Never mind walking past a few guards—now, just living takes courage. Herod & Co. are not going to be sleeping forever. Dawn is approaching. The guards back at the prison will soon discover Peter's absence. A manhunt will begin. Now that he has broken out of prison and entered the city, Peter isn't just living at the Next Level—he's a fugitive running at the Next Level!

And he's on the run without the angel. Once the city gate opens, Acts tells us, Peter and the angel "went out and went along one street, and immediately the angel departed from him" (Acts 12:10, NASB). Imagine how strange and insecure Peter may have felt at that moment. To have experienced the angel's leading, even in what Peter thought was a vision, would have been as an oasis for a leader of the persecuted church. What a relief simply to follow! Of course, Peter was never without God's leadership—the Holy Spirit was leading Peter at all times. But here, Peter was following a discernible heavenly being; and now, after having tasted that kind of security—even if the experience did have a surreal quality to it—Peter is left in a perilous setting, seemingly alone.

There are seasons in our lives when God walks so closely with us, when His Word becomes so real to us, that we feel almost the way Peter must have felt in the presence of the angel—as if we are being led step by step; as if our steps literally are being "ordered" by God, as David wrote in the Psalms (Psalm 37:23, NKJV). Then, we reach a point where things seem to shift; the angel leaves us and we have to go on. "Now, go walk in My plans for you," we sense God saying. It isn't that God has left us. He doesn't quit ordering our steps; He doesn't quit talking to us. We've just entered a different stretch of our journey in friendship with Him. Now that He has given us understanding and direction, He allows us the room to respond and determine, "Okay, where do I go from here?"

At such moments, no matter how vulnerable you may feel, you must resist the temptation to become overwhelmed by fear. After Moses died, God charged Joshua to lead the people into the Promised Land and said, "Be strong and courageous! Do not tremble or be dismayed, for the Lord your God is with you wherever you go" (Joshua 1:9, NASB). You are not alone. Do not let the enemy make you believe a lie—that God has abandoned you in this next phase of the journey and left you to make it in the city on your own. God is with you! He has plans for you. Maintain our fourth Next Level heart attitude, a heart to seek God, and keep looking to Him for guidance. Stand on His Word. Remember who you are—God's empowered friend. And be courageous.

In his coming-to moment, Peter chose to focus not on his own vulnerability but on the miracle God had performed. We read, "When Peter came to himself, he said, 'Now I know for sure that the Lord has sent forth His angel and rescued me from the hand of Herod and from all that the Jewish people were expecting' " (Acts 12:11, NASB). As Peter came to himself, his mind was not focused on his enemies—Herod and those Jews in the city who meant him harm—but on God's supernatural ability to deliver him from his enemies. "Now I know for sure," he said.

In prison, Peter could have only known by faith that God could rescue him—but faith had become sight. As you, too, wake up to the realization that God really has broken you out of limitations and brought you into the city, make a decision to keep your eyes on the God of the miraculous. Pause for a moment and stand in awe. You are in the city! This is what you longed for—you're free! Have you forgotten your battle with frustration in the prison? All of those nights crying because you just wanted out? Remember those experiences, and worship God. You found a way to worship Him in limitations, when He was making internal changes in your heart. You praised Him as He broke you out of your prison. Now, He has brought you into the city—you're finally "seeing something." Don't be shy. Give God what He deserves. Exercise our second Next Level heart attitude, a heart of gratitude to God. Thank God for where you are, and then let your amazement and gratitude build your faith in His ability to keep you as you walk on.

CHOOSING TO CONNECT

Peter's revelation about what God had done in his life determined the first choice he made in the city—where to go: "And when he realized this [that God had rescued him], he went to the house of Mary, the mother of John, who was also called Mark, where many were gathered together and were praying" (Acts 12:12, NASB).

When we come to ourselves and recognize that God has freed us, our need to connect with other people becomes more pressing. Moving forward at the Next Level is not an experience in isolation. We need people to walk with us. Once he woke up, Peter first understood where he was—disconnected from the purposes of ill-meaning people. Then, he sought to connect with people who loved him and wished him well. His "Aha!" moment was double-edged. He was saying, "Yes! The people who hate me didn't kill me, and there are people in this city who love me!" Showing himself publicly at the church was perhaps one of the riskiest things Peter could have done, but he needed his community. And you need yours.

Now that you have been released from some limitations, do you find yourself, like Peter, seeking to connect more deeply in healthy relationships? Or is connecting with people the last thing you want to do? Maybe you've been burned in the past. Maybe you've suffered rejection and pain at the hands of people. Now that you're free and walking in the city, you just want to be left alone. Is that how you feel? If so, it is certainly understandable. We've all suffered in relationships—some of us much more than others. Once we get free of certain issues in life, we can find ourselves uncertain of whether trusting people again is wise. And yet, though people hurt us, we cannot discount all people. When we become God's friends, we become part of His family (John 1:12). We are inextricably tied to others.

If you allow unhealthy or destructive relationship experiences to prevent you from connecting with people, you will struggle to walk in all of God's plans for your life. God's plans for you include people; you cannot reach your potential without them. Despite your negative experiences, there are people in this world who are safe and trustworthy—people who will care about you, pray for you, and help you become your best. As you come to yourself and move forward at the Next Level, it is God's will that you connect with such people. He will help you find them; He will be with you wherever you go. But, like Peter, you must have courage, make the choice, and, in faith, take the risk.

THE STARS IN YOUR MOVIE

Sometimes, finding trustworthy people can be a matter of taking another look at our lives. Often, we make the destructive people the stars in our movie and cast those who bless our lives as silent extras. We forget to see the safe people. We never hear them. They're just there. The only people ever speaking in our movie are the people who are hurting or discouraging us.

For a time, Herod and the people wanting to harm Peter took the lead parts in his movie; when Peter came to himself, though, and went to the church, he made a directorial change. He found a new star, a new shining star, for his movie. Her name was Rhoda, and she made her debut at the front gate.

"When he knocked at the door of the gate, a servant-girl named Rhoda came to answer. When she recognized Peter's voice, because of her joy she did not open the gate, but ran in and announced that Peter was standing in front of the gate. They said to her, 'You are out of your mind!' But she kept insisting that it was so. They kept saying, 'It is his angel.' But Peter continued knocking. And, when they had opened the door, they saw him and were amazed" (Acts 12:13-16, NASB).

Rhoda is so overwhelmed by Peter's arrival that she leaves him at the front gate to run and tell the others, "It's Peter! Quit praying—he's free!" Within moments, the others would see Peter and believe Rhoda's report, and they would be just as enthused and astonished to see their leader. Initially, however, Rhoda was the lone believer. She played a special part because she was the one who believed first.

Rhoda is the kind of person we need at the center of our lives. Rhoda recognized Peter. A "Rhoda" is someone who sees you for who you really are—someone who can see beyond your imperfections to the greatness inside of you. A Rhoda will take risks in order to support you. Once Rhoda heard Peter's voice, she insisted on his identity, even when the others called her crazy.

A Rhoda is also someone who will pray for you. The Bible says the "effective, fervent prayer" of righteous men and women accomplishes a great deal (James 5:16, NKJV). You need people in your life who share your faith and know how to pray. Even before the angel shows up to break Peter out of the prison, we read, "So Peter was kept in the prison, but prayer for him was being made fervently by the church to God" (Acts 12:5, NASB). Right there in the Acts narrative, God highlights the real stars of Peter's movie—the people supporting him in prayer.

Maybe we need to audition some of the extras in our movie and give them the starring roles. Can you think of some casting changes you need to make? Out with Herod and in with Rhoda. Out with the ill-meaning people and in with the praying people. For too long, the people causing you pain have been allowed to dominate your thought life, keep you in a state of anxiety, and dictate your decisions, while those who bless you have been given no real influence. Now that you're free of some limitations—now that you've entered the city—make a directorial change! Don't let Herod dominate your movie when you can cast an angel and a Rhoda and others who are dedicated to helping you become your best. Now that you're moving forward at the Next Level, be courageous—exercise your authority and recast that film!

BEING A RHODA

I love it when the people I pastor come to me and say, "How did you see the potential in me when I didn't see it myself?" I get to tell them that I saw their potential because I was looking for it. How did I know to look for it? Because the Rhodas in my life have taught me how to be a Rhoda to others.

The city is the place of both our freedom and our service. Just as we need Rhodas, we need to be Rhodas for those God brings to us. Being a Rhoda is part of God's plan for you and me. Life in relationship is reciprocal: we receive and we give. We receive so we can give. Once he got free, Peter returned to the community of faith not just to gain support, but, having experienced a miracle, he also showed up to give support. He needed Rhoda and the others, but the people needed their leader to take his place and make the body whole again.

As soon as Peter entered the house, he began extending himself. All of the people had come running to the door and were celebrating. Then, we read, "But motioning to them with his hand to be silent, he [Peter] described to them how the Lord had led him out of the prison. And he said, 'Report these things to James [another leader named James, probably the half-brother of Jesus] and the brethren.' Then he left and went to another place" (Acts 12:17, NASB).

What did Peter do in those brief moments at Mary's house? He calmed the people, gave his testimony, and instructed them to share his testimony with other believers. Peter encouraged the people. To encourage means to add courage. First, Peter exercised courage by going to the house and connecting. Then, by sharing what God had done to bring him out of prison, Peter added courage—he lifted the people, building them up in their faith.

Peter also encouraged himself. Encouraging others is part of the way we build courage into our own lives. The Bible says we reap what we sow (Galatians 6:7-9). As you encourage others, you become encouraged. As you share your testimony, your own faith grows. As you talk about what God is doing in your life, His plans become more real to you, and your courage to move forward in those plans increases. Can you see the blessing of a life shared with people? We help one another walk on in God's plans.

You may not be a leader of many like Peter, but there are people in your life who need you. You have the ability to make a difference in their lives. Some of my Rhodas have made the difference in my life. My parents, though both of them have gone to be with the Lord, remain my greatest cheerleaders. They always believed in me with such passion that, even when I failed or didn't receive the recognition they thought I deserved, I was buoyed with hope and the courage to try again. My pastor, Bishop Richard Hilton, has been my friend for more than 20 years, and he often still closes our conversations saying, "Court, you're the best." At times, I find myself weeping over his words. How is it that, when I don't feel so great about me, he still believes in me? Then, there is my Rhoda of Rhodas—my wife, Janeen. Since I was 17 years old, she has been there for me—loving me through difficult times, cheering me on when no one else could, and standing by, ready to support my dreams. I'm not sure what I did to deserve that kind of love, but I'm so grateful I have it. And those whom you will love and encourage will feel just as grateful for you.

EMPTYING AND STAYING FULFILLED

The time to start pouring into the lives of others is always now. You don't have to have everything together to begin loving, serving, and building people up—Peter was just out of his chains, on the run, wearing the same clothes as when he was arrested. He had been walking around in a dreamlike state for who knows how long, and probably didn't have much of a plan. But he stopped at Mary's house. He encouraged the believers there; he told them to pass along his story to others. Then, he left for another place, probably to share his story again. In beleaguered form, Peter released encouragement not just to a few people, but to several groups of them. He didn't just add courage—he multiplied it.

Only minutes out of prison yourself, you may feel weary and off-kilter. Are you struggling to find your footing in the city? Are you unclear about where you're heading and not even close to being on top of your game? Even in your shaky condition, you can still begin adding value to other people. Like Peter, you can stop and encourage others. You have something to share.

Just think about how far you've come. Flip back to the Mile Marker and Charting Your Course features at the end of each chapter in this book and review the arc of your journey. You've walked through some limitations. You've learned how to release frustration and practice contentment in difficulty. You've seen God shine a light in your life when it should've been dark. You've exercised the faith to get up when you were chained down. You've put on your clothes and shoes, walking through a preparation period for life "on the outside." You've dared to walk past your old issues, your first and second guards, believing God would shut down their influence in your life. You've walked up to the city gate, faced that formidable barrier, and watched as God pushed it open. And you've gone in—you've entered the city! Now, you're coming to yourself, digging deep for courage, and recognizing all that God has done for you. You have something to share!

Not only that—you also have the resources you need in order to keep sharing. As we give ourselves to loving and encouraging others, God will give us everything we need to keep doing it. We may feel drained, empty, and a little worse for wear; but in God, our supply does not run out. Jesus said of himself, "The Son of Man did not come to be served, but to serve, and to give His life a ransom for many" (Matthew 20:28, NASB). Jesus lived to give Himself away, and God gave Him overwhelming resources to finish the work.

You can see the fullness of Jesus when He gets ready to feed 5,000 people. He doesn't need much to do it—just a few fish and loaves of bread—because He is so full of resources Himself (Matthew 14:13-21). When Jesus walks on water during the storm to get to His disciples' boat, He is so full of life the sea can't swallow him (Matthew 14:22-33). The life in Jesus is so overpowering that, before He raises His friend, Lazarus, from the dead, He says to Martha, "I am the resurrection and the life" (John 11:25, NASB). On the cross, Jesus has to allow Himself to die, because He is so full of life in order to fulfill His purpose that only He can let that life go (Luke 23:46; John 10:17-18).

Jesus experienced fulfillment as He was emptied. Emptying was an expression of His love for the Father; God's response, keeping Jesus full, was an expression of His love for His Son. This was the way they lived in friendship when Jesus was on earth—in perfect reciprocity. Jesus gave all, and God gave all. And that is what our friendship journey with God is designed to look like: a picture of unhindered intimacy, transparency, and exchange. In love, we give God all—we empty ourselves, we serve others, we use our lives to bring others life. And in love, God gives us all, keeping us full of His Spirit and providing what we need to walk on and keep giving.

Jesus told His disciples, "For whoever wishes to save his life will lose it; but whoever loses his life for My sake will find it" (Matthew 16:25, NASB). Fulfillment at the Next Level comes as we love God and lose ourselves in love for God. The world says, "Fill yourself." That is a striving mentality and only perpetuates frustration. But Jesus says, "Give yourself." Giving is both the expression of our fulfillment in God and also the way to ongoing fulfillment in Him, for only as you give your life will you find it.

ADDING COURAGE

So, how do we do it? Now that we've come through some phases of our journey and gained more understanding about what living at the Next Level is all about, how do we prepare ourselves to continue on in God's plans, adding courage to others as we go? Let's take another look at some of the principles that shape our Next Level experience. Even before we reach out to others, we build courage into our own hearts as we remember the truths that have changed us to this point.

What we can see, we can help others see. What we can say to ourselves, we can articulate to others.

Friendship with God Is the Next Level

Here is the foundation of everything we've learned: God made us to be His friends. He made us for love. Loving God is our primary purpose. Our friendship with Him is our Next Level—the place where we find true fulfillment. We can get off track in life waiting for some spectacular breakthrough, some big miracle moment when we finally "arrive" and all of our dreams come true. The moment we choose God's friendship, we arrive. Becoming God's friend is our breakthrough. Rather than striving in frustration to get to what we imagine is the "next level," we need to focus on learning how to live at the real Next Level—in friendship with God.

Living at the Next Level Is Journeying in Friendship with God

Life in God is complex, diverse, and dynamic. It is a journey, a process—as David wrote, a "path of life" (Psalm 16:11, NIV). Our terrain and experiences on the path constantly vary. There are hard climbs and times of refreshment. People come and go. Our circumstances turn unexpectedly. Our hearts change. We collapse in exhaustion. We get thrown in prison. We break out of prison. We gain and we lose. We fight battles and experience blessings. We enter the city. We veer off the path. We lose the path. But God brings us back. This is living at the Next Level—life in all of its rich diversity, lived as a journey in friendship with God.

Fulfillment Is Available in Every Phase of the Journey

Fulfillment comes in knowing God. Because we were made for intimacy, there is nothing outside of relationship with God that can satisfy us completely. In Christ, Paul wrote, "you have been made complete" (Colossians 2:10, NASB). Part of living at the Next Level is learning to enjoy the journey and experience the fulfillment of walking in friendship with God every day.

God designed your journey uniquely for you—no one else has a journey like yours. Whether sweating it out in prison, getting dressed so you can break out, walking past some old guards, or going free in the city, you are on a "designer journey" that God is using to open up springs of intimacy between you and Him. You have access to God's intimacy at all times, in every phase of your journey, and your periods of deepest frustration can be opportunities for your sweetest experiences of intimacy and growth. This is the way you transform your life's frustrations into fulfillment—by living in love with God.

The Friendship Journey Is a Walk of Faith

Paul wrote, "We walk by faith, not by sight" (2 Corinthians 5:7, NASB). Faith is the basis of our friendship with God: Accepting God's forgiveness and love requires faith. Our friendship journey with God is a faith walk. At every phase, we exercise faith. In prison, we live in faith that our Friend is working for our good. By faith, we see ourselves the way God sees us—not as prisoners, but as free. When God says, "Get up, it's time to break out," we engage our faith and make the decision to try, even if getting up looks impossible. In faith, we prepare ourselves for change, practicing a lifestyle of obedience.

We transition from one phase of the journey to another in faith, following God in the dark, walking past old issues, relationships, and challenges that used to hinder us. By faith, we walk through gates of change and opportunity that God opens, and we enter the city. We connect with other people in faith, allowing Rhodas into our life and extending ourselves as Rhodas to others. Everything about life in God requires faith, and we have that faith. God has given us the "measure of faith," and we build it up as we stay in His Word, growing in our friendship with Him (Romans 12:3, NASB).

KEEPING YOUR HEART HEALTHY

Walking on at the Next Level will require constant attention to your heart. Keeping your heart healthy is the way you build stamina for the journey. The phases of the journey with God are fluid, unpredictable, and overlapping. You may find yourself freed from limitations and walking in the city in one area of life and on the front end of a brand new prison sentence in another area. If you don't tend to your heart as you go, the ups and downs of life can slow your pace or, worse, incapacitate you (Proverbs 4:23).

We've focused on four heart attitudes in this book. In different phases of our journey, some of these stand out more prominently than others; but all of them work together to keep us growing in God on the path of life. If you haven't already, go ahead and memorize them; as you encourage yourself in these attitudes, you also equip yourself to strengthen the hearts of others along the way.

Next Level Heart Attitudes
1. A Heart for Friendship with God
2. A Heart of Gratitude to God
3. A Heart of Expectancy Toward God
4. A Heart to Seek God

A Heart for Friendship with God

Jesus said the greatest commandment is this: "And you shall love the Lord your God with all your heart, and with all your soul, and with all your mind, and with all your strength" (Mark 12:30, NASB). There is a depth of intimacy available to you in God that has no limits, no borders around it. Satan knows this; he doesn't want you to have that intimacy. But it is yours. Jesus says, "Behold, I stand at the door and knock; if anyone hears My voice and opens the door, I will come in to him and will dine with him, and he with Me" (Revelation 3:20, NASB). God makes Himself completely available to you. Is loving Him your heart's priority? A heart for His friendship is the first heart attitude you must cultivate and maintain on your journey.

A Heart of Gratitude to God

The psalmist wrote, "Enter His gates with thanksgiving and His courts with praise" (Psalm 100:4, NASB). Expressing gratitude to God is the way we approach God, and one of the ways we love Him.

Gratitude builds intimacy. As we thank God for who He is—a mighty, loving, faithful God—our anxiety subsides, and resting in Him becomes easier. We also maintain our faith as we cultivate a heart of gratitude. Thanking God for what He has already done in our lives builds our faith for what He can do, both in our present distress and in the future. In faith, we can then thank God for what He will do, even before we see any change. Our gratitude becomes an expression of trust, and trust is the bedrock of friendship.

A Heart of Expectancy Toward God

When Moses questioned God's ability, God responded, "Is the Lord's power too little?" (Numbers 11:23, NASB) God is supernatural. He can do anything He chooses at any time. In the struggles of life, we can forget this. We forget who God is—the Creator—and, in discouragement, we cease to expect Him to move in our lives. A heart of expectancy toward God flows out of our faith in Him. Because we believe our Friend, we expect Him to keep His Word, to work in our circumstances, to stay with us, and to give us guidance. Cultivating a heart of expectancy toward God is one way we protect our friendship with Him. When our expectation wanes, we can drift away from God. But as we choose to place our trust in Him, we will find ourselves better able to rest, release our frustration, and enjoy the gift of loving Him.

A Heart to Seek God

So often in life, we do not understand where our path is leading. How do we journey with God when we can't discern where to go? The

Bible promises us God will lead us. In Proverbs, we read, "Trust in the Lord with all your heart and do not lean on your own understanding. In all your ways acknowledge Him, and He will make your paths straight" (Proverbs 3:5-6, NASB). When we feel lost or in the dark, we must make a decision to seek our Friend in faith, believing that He wants us to know His will. Jesus promised that, if we will seek, and keep seeking, we will find (Matthew 7:7). More than seeking God just for answers, we seek Him for Himself. We seek God because we long for Him and desire His intimacy above all else. Like the beloved in the Song of Solomon, when we find our Friend, we hold on to Him and do not let go. In His presence, we find everything our hearts long for and need.

WALK ON

"Now when day came," we read in Acts, "there was no small disturbance among the soldiers as to what could have become of Peter. When Herod had searched for him and had not found him, he examined the guards and ordered that they be led away to execution" (Acts 12:18-19, NASB).

There are some limitations and issues in life that, once the Lord finishes with them, are finished for good. Herod could not find Peter in the morning. The guards who once held Peter were removed and executed. Herod died soon afterward, and Peter moved on in his journey, no longer deterred by those foes. What was going on at the end of the story? In short, Peter was walking in friendship with God, just as he had been all along. Peter operated in faith—exercising courage, connecting with others, and moving forward—and God met

Peter's faith, shutting down the negative influences that once had the power to hold and destroy him.

God can work the same way in your life today. Some of your struggles and limitations have run their course—God is finished with them. Those guards are dead. Herod will never find you. You are free from those old issues. Certainly, there will be new guards. After Herod executed the old guards, presumably, he hired some more. You will face more issues, obstacles, and limitations on your journey. But in some areas of life, God has released you to move forward, and those old issues can no longer hold sway over you.

This is a time to engage your faith. Remember God's words to Joshua: "Be strong and courageous!" God is with you. He has brought you this far—into the city. Expect Him to fulfill His good plans for your life. As you journey on, have the courage to stop by Mary's house and encourage those who are languishing in their own limitations. They need to hear what God has done for you. They need to hear about the riches of His friendship, the dynamic journey with God available to them, the fulfillment that comes in walking with God, and the ability to walk by faith.

You can tell them. Like Peter, you can add courage, because now, you know for sure that God Himself has brought you out of your prison. You know what God can do. You know Him. Be encouraged! Maintain your Next Level heart attitudes as you go: Love God with all that you are. Stay grateful to Him. Expect Him to work in your life. Seek Him, and keep seeking. And in all of this, enjoy the journey— enjoy it! This is your life. Right where you are, as God's friend, you are living at the Next Level. Have faith, be courageous, and walk on!

Mapping Your Next Level Leadership Journey

MILE MARKER: WHERE AM I ON THE JOURNEY?

In what areas of your leadership are you coming to yourself and realizing that certain limitations are being removed?

_____

_____

Are you discovering that you are walking out of some prisons that were created to establish deeper friendship with God?

_____

_____

Do you see any opportunity for more effective leadership now that you have passed certain barriers?

_____

_____

Let this phase of the journey be filled with gratitude for the amazing way that God has orchestrated your life!

This week, keep an eye out for others who need the encouragement of your testimony. Many of your colleagues are likely in similar places as you have been.

CHARTING YOUR COURSE: FOCUSING ON THE PATH AHEAD

We talked about the role of Rhoda in Peter's deliverance. She recognized him immediately when he arrived at the prayer meeting. Who do you have in your life that recognizes God's plan and purpose for you? It could be a spouse, colleague, friend, leader or a life coach; but we desperately need Rhodas. Begin to look for yours because, once you're out of your limitations, you will need affirmation of who you truly are.

Ask Him to help you connect with those who can strengthen your heart during the next steps and help guide you further. Remember, it's about friendship with God, so keep that at the forefront of your heart and mind. Out of an overflowing friendship with God will come an exuberant, renewed passion to serve and lead.

LEADER'S PRAYER: ASKING FOR GUIDANCE

"Lord, I am ready to obey Your direction for my life. Thank You for speaking to me so profoundly through this book, and help me to remain committed to the process. In Jesus' name, amen."

LEADER'S WORD: RECEIVING GUIDANCE FROM HIS WORD

"As iron sharpens iron, so a friend sharpens a friend." —*Proverbs 27:17 (NLT)*

ACKNOWLEDGMENTS

I would like to take the time to acknowledge some very special people who were critical to the process of writing this book. Stacy Mattingly, who is the best collaborative writer on the planet. Wes Yoder, president of Ambassador Speakers Bureau & Literary Agency, whose dedication to me and to this book has impacted me deeply. Dr. James Flynn, Regent University School of Divinity, who provided critical scholarly assistance in the editing process. Terry Webb, our ministry's marketing director, whose planning and promotion brilliance illuminated the process.

The pastoral team, staff, and members of Calvary Revival Church in Norfolk, Virginia; the staff of BCM Ministries; and the pastors and leaders of Calvary Alliance of Churches and Ministries. Your support has given me the courage to write while maintaining all the other responsibilities given me, and I am forever grateful.

Pastor Kingsley Appiagyei and the congregation of Trinity Baptist Church in London, England, where I first preached about Peter and his Acts 12 miracle. Thank you for receiving the Word!

My pastors, Richard and Theresa Hilton, who have been my friends for more than twenty years; and every pastor, friend, teacher, classmate, and acquaintance who helped facilitate my success in the journey of life and in the wonderful journey of friendship with God.

The people in my life who make life worth living—my family. To my children: C.J., Lydia and David, Benjamin, Alexander, and Xavier. Thank you for praying for me and for putting up with my long writing hours, short attention span, and all it took to complete this project. To my "little" sister, Tamala, for following me to Disney World and everywhere else I've gone! A special thank you to my extended family for always believing in me.

Finally, and most importantly, to my wife of more than 30 years, Janeen. Thank you for standing beside me. I love you.

CLAIM YOUR FREE
ANNUAL SUBSCRIPTION

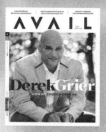

AT AVAILJOURNAL.COM

($59 VALUE)

A V A I L +

AVAIL LEADERSHIP PODCAST

WITH VIRGIL SIERRA

FOLLOW THE LEADER

STAY CONNECTED